He Leads Me Beside Still Waters

He Leads Me Beside Still Waters

A Forty-Day Journey Toward Rest for Your Soul

Jennifer Kennedy Dean

BROADMAN
&HOLMAN
PUBLISHERS

Nashville, Tennessee

0-8054-2379-6

Published by Broadman & Holman Publishers, Nashville, Tennessee

Published in association with the literary agency of Alive Communications, Inc.,
7680 Goddard St., Suite 200, Colorado Springs, CO 80920

Dewey Decimal Classification: 242
Subject Heading: MEDITATIONS / PERSONAL RETREATS
Library of Congress Card Catalog Number: 00-067470

Unless otherwise indicated, all Scripture references are from The Holy Bible, New International Version (NIV), copyright © 1973, 1978, 1984 by International Bible Society. Other versions cited include the NASB, the New American Standard Bible, © the Lockman Foundation, 1960, 1962, 1963, 1968, 1971, 1972, 1973, 1975, 1978, used by permission.

Library of Congress Cataloging-in-Publication Data

Dean, Jennifer Kennedy.
     He leads me beside still waters : a forty-day journey toward rest for your soul /
Jennifer Kennedy Dean.
          p.   cm.
     Includes bibliographical references
     ISBN 0-8054-2379-6 (pbk.)
     1. Meditations.   2. Retreats.   I. Title
     BV4832.2.D395   2001
     242—dc21
                                                                            00-067470
                                                                            CIP

1 2 3 4 5 6 7 8 9 10 05 04 03 02 01

Contents

Dedication

*To my mother,
who has lived her life in a soul-sabbath,
and whose legacy is peace.*

Acknowledgments

Every one of my books is a Dean family project.
Thank you, Wayne.
Thank you, Brantley, Kennedy, and Stinson.

Without your generous and unstinting support,
this book would not exist.

I love your wild humor and I love your
unrestrained passion for Christ.

Preface

For as long as I can remember, I have had a deep interest in prayer. As a college student, I moved into a more mature commitment to Christ, and that deep interest grew to be a consuming passion. Every day I cry out for insight and "call aloud for understanding" (Prov. 2:3) about how prayer works. I know that prayer is the key to the kingdom.

Over these years, the one truth that has fallen into place and caused all the pieces to fit is this: God is not calling us to "a prayer life." He is calling us to "a praying life." He is not calling us to an activity. He is calling us to a relationship.

A praying life is open to the power and provision of God. The focus of a praying life is always "How do I keep my life available to the Spirit?"

A praying life moves you into a dimension of living where your daily, minute-by-minute experience is walking in the flow of God's provision. You are met at every step with the progressive unfolding of His tailor-made plan for your life (Eph. 2:10). You cease your struggle to find the will of God because the will of God has found you. Every moment is pregnant with purpose. Every moment is drenched in power. I can't find the words to say it all! Prayer is no longer the means by which you attempt to get God to perform for you and becomes, instead, the means by which you connect with His heart and mind. A praying life is a life of peace and soul-rest.

Here's the secret: the praying life is Jesus. He lives in you. He is longing to express His Praying Life through you. He is the one and only Praying Life, and He is living in you. Here is how Andrew Murray expresses it:

> We do this because we are partakers of His life—"Christ is
> our life"; "No longer I, but Christ liveth in me." The life in
> Him and in us is one and the same. His life in heaven is an
> ever-praying life. When it descends and takes possession of us,

in us, too, it is an ever-praying life—a life that without ceasing asks and receives from God. . . . As we know that Jesus communicates His whole life in us, He also, out of that prayerfulness which is His alone, breathes into us our praying.[1]

Jesus says that when we learn from Him, we will find rest for our souls. What did those who observed Him day by day, minute by minute, recognize as the key to His joy, His confidence, and His soul-rest?

"One day Jesus was praying in a certain place. When he finished, one of his disciples said to him, 'Lord, teach us to pray'" (Luke 11:1).

He is the Prayer Teacher. Do you long for soul-rest? Do you yearn for peace? Then ask Him now, "Lord, teach me to pray."

"If you call out for insight and cry aloud for understanding, and if you look for it as for silver and search for it as for hidden treasure, then you will understand the fear of the LORD and find the knowledge of God. For the LORD gives wisdom, and from his mouth come knowledge and understanding" (Prov. 2:3–6).

SECTION 1
BEGINNINGS

*The Father wants to take you by the hand and lead you into
His rest. . . . He wants to teach you that Sabbath is not just a
day of the week but, more importantly, a state of the soul.
He wants you to know the secret of living in a soul-sabbath.*

Invitation

*"Come to me, all you who are weary and burdened, and
I will give you rest. Take my yoke upon you and learn from me,
for I am gentle and humble in heart, and you will find rest
for your souls. For my yoke is easy and my burden is light."*
(Matt. 11:28–30)

Rest for your soul. Let the words wrap themselves around your heart. *Rest for your soul.* Let the promise flow into your inmost being and take up residence there. *Rest for your soul.*

Learn from Jesus. As you learn more and more about who He is, you will find anxiety losing its hold on you; you will find bitterness, anger, and defensiveness retreating; you will find uncertainty and fear yielding to boldness and stoutheartedness. In Him is an unending "soul-sabbath."

Just as the nation of Israel journeyed to the Promised Land, the land of rest, you also can begin a journey, the destination of which is soul-rest. Will you take the first step of your journey? Right now, as you commit yourself to learning from Him, you have embarked on the way. You are taking hold of the promise and you are trusting the promiser. A promise is only as good as the one who makes it. You can rely on a promise when you know you can trust the promiser. Jesus Himself has given you His word. Learn from Him, and your soul *will* find rest.

Are anxiety, fear, and stress your constant companions? Does uncertainty dog your way? Are you plagued with feelings of insecurity? Is your soul in a state of turmoil? The Father wants to take you by the hand and lead you into His rest, just as He took Israel by the hand to lead her out of Egypt and unto the Land of Rest (Jer. 31:32). He wants to teach you that Sabbath is not a day of the week but a state of the soul. He wants you to know the secret of living in a soul-sabbath.

Let this book be a resource for your journey. Commit yourself to forty days of a single-minded, determined pursuit of the only One who can satisfy your craving for peace. Learn what it means to live in "sabbath." We'll explore the deeper meanings of the word *sabbath* and also learn how to set aside sabbath moments each day to delight fully in the Lord.

What is "sabbath-rest"?

The Old Covenant (Old Testament) is a book of shadows, the substance of which is revealed in the New Covenant. Everything recorded in the Old Covenant Scriptures is true and accurate. The events recorded there really happened, and the spiritual principles are authentic, but running through the whole document is another layer of truth. Everything points to Jesus. Jesus is central in every page of the Old Covenant: He is the substance whose shadow is cast from Genesis through Malachi. As we begin to look for the substance of the "sabbath-rest" in the Old Covenant, keep this principle in mind: a shadow is a one-dimensional drawing of the reality. It is not the whole picture. It is a signpost pointing to the reality.

Another interpretive principle for you to apply is this: The natural laws upon which the material world functions are a model and a graphic of spiritual reality. "For since the creation of the world God's invisible qualities—his eternal power and divine nature—have been clearly seen, being understood from what has been made" (Rom. 1:20). The material realm (earth) and the spiritual realm (heaven) are not two separate worlds, but instead are two ends of one continuum.

> What if earth
> Be but the shadow of heaven and things therein
> Each to other like more than on earth is thought?
> —Milton

This is exactly the cumulative evidence of Scripture. As we look at sabbath-rest from the earth-perspective, we will let the Spirit of God show us its ultimate meaning. We'll search for the substance. To understand the inner workings of sabbath-rest, we will examine three Hebrew concepts, all ingredients of an uninterrupted inner tranquility: sabbath, rest, and peace.

What is God's rest?

In interpreting Scripture there is a commonly held principle referred to as "the law of the first mention." At the first mention of an idea, certain foundational truths are introduced, upon which further revelation will build. In looking for the deeper meanings of the Word, I try to start with the first mention. For sabbath, the first mention is in Genesis 2:1–3. Because I want the language to be an exact translation from the original Hebrew, I quote this passage from *The Five Books of Moses* by Everett Fox. The English wording is slightly awkward, but it is true to the Hebrew.

> Thus were finished the heavens and the earth, with all of their array. God had finished, on the seventh day, his work that he had made, and then he ceased, on the seventh day, from all his work that he had made. God gave the seventh day his blessing, and he hallowed it, for on it he ceased from all his work, that by creating, God had made.[2]

The Hebrew word that Fox translated "ceased" is the word *shabath.* The word in English is *sabbath.* In most of our translations, the word has been translated "rest." In Genesis 2:2, then, we find that God "sabbathed."

Several words here describe how God sabbathed: *finished, ceased,* and *hallowed.* Notice that Fox translated *shabath* as "cease" rather than "rest." This is truer to its meaning. According to Edward Mahler, *shabath* means "to be complete" rather than "to rest."[3]

The Hebrew word most often used for "rest" is the word *menuha.* It means more than an absence of activity. It means "a settled, deep stillness." It means "to be relaxed in body and soul." The opposite of this kind of rest is restlessness. *Menuha* is the sabbath-rest we seek.

Rabbi Abraham Joshua Heschel wrote:

> The words "On the seventh day God finished His work" (Genesis 2:2) seem to be a puzzle. Is it not said: "He rested on

the seventh day"? "In six days the LORD made heaven and earth" (Exodus 20:11)? We would surely expect the Bible to tell us that on the sixth day God finished His work. Obviously, the ancient rabbis concluded, there was an act of creation on the seventh day. Just as heaven and earth were created in six days, *menuha* was created on the Sabbath.

"After the six days of creation—what did the universe still lack? *Menuha*. Came the Sabbath, came *menuha*, and the universe was complete."

Menuha, which we usually render with "rest," means here much more than withdrawal from labor and exertion, more than freedom from toil, strain, or activity of any kind. *Menuha* is not a negative concept but something real and intrinsically positive. This must have been the view of the ancient rabbis if they believed that it took a special act of creation to bring it into being, that the universe would be incomplete without it.[4]

At the first mention of *shabath*, we find that God completed His work of creating, that He ceased His creating, and that He hallowed or sanctified the day because of its significance to Him. God's rest, not humankind's rest, identifies the Sabbath. We can plausibly speculate with the ancient rabbis that on this first Sabbath, God deliberately created for His people a gift—the gift of *menuha*, rest. We can be at rest because God did the work. When He set Adam and Eve in the garden, the place was a finished work. It was complete. It was a land of rest.

God had another gift for His creation, the gift of *shalom*, a Hebrew word usually translated in English as "peace." It means "total well-being." It means "wholeness and health in body and soul." It means "complete." *Shalom* and *shabath* are related, and both suggest the meaning of "finished."

Why did God rest?
Draw on these thoughts to see the true meaning of *sabbath*. Scripture records in Exodus 20:10–11, for example, that God rested on the seventh

day. Why did God rest? Had He exhausted Himself? The Scripture is clear: God rested because He was finished. He was finished with all of His work, so He sabbathed. He ceased. The word *sabbath* means "to be finished; to have completed the work."

God created for six days, and then He sabbathed. For how long did He sabbath? Did He pick up where He'd left off when Day Eight dawned? God, on the seventh day of creation, began a sabbath that was to last forever. "And yet his work has been finished since the creation of the world" (Heb. 4:3b).

God's work has been in a finished state, completed, since Day Seven. When was the Lamb slain? Before the world began (Rev. 13:8). When were the names of those who would be saved written in the book of life? Before the world began (Rev. 17:8; Eph. 1:4). When was the kingdom prepared for believers? Before the world began (Matt. 25:34). Look at 2 Thessalonians 2:13; 2 Timothy 1:9; Titus 1:1–2; and Ephesians 2:10. All of His work was finished, and so He sabbathed.

Yet Jesus stated, "'My Father is always at his work to this very day, and I, too, am working'" (John 5:17). At one level, everything is finished. God's work in its finished state is on the spiritual end of the continuum. The work left to do is to release it into the material end of the continuum in the fullness of time.

> This grace was given us in Christ Jesus before the beginning of time, but it has now been revealed through the appearing of our Savior, Christ Jesus, who has destroyed death and has brought life and immortality to light through the gospel. (2 Tim. 1:9b–10)

Do you see what this means? The action—grace was given us in Christ Jesus—was completed before the beginning of time. But God revealed it in Christ's coming to earth. God's work is finished, but it will be revealed on the earth at its ripe and appointed moment.

Hold this thought. We'll return to it and expand on it later. First, let's put some of the other pieces in place.

What are the Sabbath shadows?

The Sabbath Day Observance

God established the Sabbath day, the seventh day of each week, to be set aside for rest from work and for delighting in the Lord. The Sabbath observance is a day on which His people are to mimic His rest. We are to enter into peaceful tranquility, the perpetual state of the Father. The scientific community provides ample proof that regular rest from work is necessary for the mental and physical well-being of persons, animals, and land. The observance of the Sabbath-rest is beneficial to the physical world and provides for its optimum functioning. But the physical and mental rest of the Sabbath observance is only a shadow of the real rest and soul-sabbath that God has made available to His people. Let me say again, sabbath is not ultimately a day of the week, but a state of the soul.

The Land of Rest

The next shadow-figure of sabbath-rest is the Promised Land. The *menuha* in the Garden of Eden was disrupted by the entrance of sin. It began as a land of rest, but became a place of labor, turmoil, and death. When God promised His people a land of their own, He called it a land of rest *(menuha)*. Part of the gift of land was the gift of rest. "Come into Canaan. Here, I will give you rest," is essentially the invitation of Yaweh to His people.

> You are not to do as we do here today, everyone as he sees fit, since you have not yet reached the *resting place* and the inheritance the LORD your God is giving you. But you will cross the Jordan and settle in the land the LORD your God is giving you as an inheritance, and *he will give you rest* from all your enemies around you so that you will live in safety. (Deut. 12:8–10, italics added)

> "Praise be to the LORD, who *has given rest* to his people Israel just as he promised. Not one word has failed of all the good

promises he gave through his servant Moses." (1 Kings 8:56, italics added)

The Promised Land, the land of Canaan, the homeland, was to be a land of rest. Rest from enemies, rest from uncertainty, rest from striving. Physical rest and soul rest. In the land of Canaan, God's people could live in His rest. When the nation of Israel refused to enter the land because of fear, God said of them:

> For forty years I was angry with that generation;
>   I said, "They are a people whose hearts go astray,
>   and they have not known my ways."
> So I declared on oath in my anger,
>   "They shall never enter *my rest.*" (Ps. 95:10–11, italics added)

At this point, then, we have sabbath (God's rest), celebrated and remembered by a weekly observance and represented by a land. Sabbath is God's rest into which His people may enter. Canaan is His rest. When His people entered Canaan, it was God's intent that they enter a land where the work had been finished.

> When the LORD your God brings you into the land he swore to your fathers, to Abraham, Isaac and Jacob, to give you—a land with large, flourishing cities you did not build, houses filled with all kinds of good things you did not provide, wells you did not dig, and vineyards and olive groves you did not plant— then when you eat and are satisfied, be careful that you do not forget the LORD. (Deut. 6:10–12a)

Canaan in the material realm is a geographical location. At the other end of the continuum, in the spiritual realm, it is Jesus Himself. The Promised Land is the shadow of the Promised One.

The writer of Hebrews connected these pictures, making them one thought: Sabbath, Canaan, God's rest, and Jesus. In Hebrews 3:16–4:10, the writer makes the case as follows. This is my summary of this passage:

Quoting Psalm 95:7–11, the writer reminded his readers of "the rebellion" or "the testing." The incident referred to is found in Exodus 17:1–7 when the Israelites complained against God and against Moses because there was no water. Having seen God provide miraculously for their every single need, they still did not trust God to meet their new needs as they arose. This is when God swore that this generation would never enter *His rest* (Canaan). The Israelites did not experience the rest of Canaan because of their unbelief. They trusted their own perceptions more than they trusted God's Word.

The writer immediately moved the analogy to the present, in essence warning readers: Don't let the same thing happen to you. You can experience Christ (the real Canaan) if you operate in faith as need enters your life (Heb. 3:7–19).

The same good news of a promised rest has been given to us. The Israelites' promise was Canaan; our promise is Jesus. They did not partake of the rest because the promise they received was not combined with faith—they did not act confidently on the promise. But the promise still remains. We can enter into the rest, and, in fact, those who have believed have entered the Promised Land, the place of rest—Jesus (4:1–3).

The Scripture tells us that God rested on the seventh day; then it says, "'They shall never enter my rest,'" tying God's sabbath-rest to the Promised Land (4:4–5). Then, "For if Joshua had given them rest [in Canaan], God would not have spoken later about another day. There remains, then, a Sabbath-rest for the people of God; for anyone who enters God's rest also rests from his own work, just as God did from his" (Heb. 4:8–10).

Again, God's own eternal sabbath, based on His finished work, was pictured by Canaan. Just as the Israelites could enter Canaan, we can "enter God's rest." Jesus is Canaan. Jesus is the finished work. Jesus is sabbath. Jesus is rest.

What does sabbath mean for us?

Sabbath for you and me means living our lives in absolute surrender and total trust in the finished work of Christ. Not only is the salvation work finished in Him, but every need that comes into our lives has already been provided for; every dilemma has already been resolved; every question has already been answered. We simply have to place our lives in the flow of His provision. Simply abide in Christ. Simply live where the power is operating. Faith-born obedience puts us in the land where the soul has continual sabbath-rest. Hear Him say, "Come to Me. You will find rest for your soul."

I wanted to take the time to lay out the whole picture. This will be central to your forty-day journey. You are headed for the Promised Land where continual, uninterrupted sabbath-rest awaits you. This is your destiny. It belongs to you. The more you learn of Him, the easier it will be to rest in Him.

Committing to a Daily Sabbath Pause

What is a "Sabbath Pause"?

The purpose of the weekly Sabbath observance was to stop everything else and take delight in the Lord; to have no other purpose or thought except to enjoy His presence and to give Him pleasure. Suppose that you committed a time each *day* for honoring the eternal Sabbath. For these forty days, let your daily time with Him be a Sabbath Pause, a time to celebrate the relationship you have with Him. Set aside a time of your day and consider it holy, set apart, sanctified. Several times in Scripture,

God described the Sabbath as a sign of the relationship between Him and His people. The soul-sabbath that He has provided for you in Christ is His sign to you of how deep His love is for you. Let the Sabbath Pause that you set aside be your sign to Him of how much you love Him.

What time is best for a Sabbath Pause?
Commit to a time frame and a schedule that is realistic for you. I encourage you, if just for these forty days, to make that time early morning. Throughout the Old Covenant, God claimed the "firsts." The firstfruits—the first of the crop (Exod. 23:16); the firstborn, both sons and animals—were to belong to the Lord (Exod. 13:2). The Father doesn't want your "seconds;" He wants your "firsts." Will you offer to Him the first of your day?

Don't let this be a discouragement to you. You may have health or scheduling issues that keep you from being able to be up early. If it is possible for you, consider whether the Lord is asking for the firstfruits of your day.

What tools do I need for my Sabbath Pause?
Design your Sabbath Pauses according to what appeals to you and is conducive to worship for you. Essentials are your Bible, a prayer journal, and a writing utensil. Other tools might be:

- devotional book
- sketch pad and pencils
- worshipful music and something to play it on
- recordings of nature sounds
- candles
- a hymn or chorus book

In Jewish life, the Sabbath day is the highlight of the week. The six days that lead up to it are preparation for it. The week and its activities revolve around the Sabbath. Consider the time in your day that you set aside for delighting fully in the Lord as the highlight of your day. Make special preparation for it. Welcome it as the Israelites welcomed the Sabbath day, and as the Jewish people do today.

How can I use body posture to express worship during my Sabbath Pause?

One of the benefits of a private, personal Sabbath Pause is that you can be completely uninhibited in your worship style. Because you are alone, you won't have to consider whether your expressions of worship will be distracting to someone else. You won't have to worry about what someone else might think of your worship. You may find yourself free to worship in ways that will help you express your openness to God's power in deeper ways.

In many ways, we use our bodies to communicate emotions. A person's body language can often communicate at a deeper level than conversation alone allows. The Scripture describes numerous postures of worship. Perhaps you will find it refreshing to physically assume some of these worship postures; or perhaps you will find it more conducive to prayer if you imagine yourself in a worship posture. Letting your body express worship is another way to show your delight in the Lord.

Consider some of these scriptural worship postures:

- Kneel in His presence.
    Come, let us bow down in worship,
       let us kneel before the LORD our Maker. (Ps. 95:6)
- Spread out your hands toward heaven.
    I spread out my hands to you;
       my soul thirsts for you like a parched land. (Ps. 143:6)
- Lift up your hands.
    Lift up your hands in the sanctuary
       and praise the LORD. (Ps. 134:2)
- Stand before Him.
    Who may ascend the hill of the LORD?
    Who may stand in his holy place? (Ps. 24:3)

- Fall on your face before Him.

   When I saw him, I fell at his feet as though dead. (Rev. 1:17)

Using the Forty-Day *He Leads Me Beside Still Waters* Plan

In the following pages, you will find forty daily meditations, reflection questions, and journaling exercises. I challenge you to commit to forty days of daily Sabbath Pauses, ending with an optional extended retreat experience, which section 3 details. Make this commitment alone, or ask others to make the commitment with you.

The devotional material is divided into seven-day segments, with five days of readings per week. Every sixth day of each segment will be reflective exercises and thought-probing questions. Every seventh day will be a day for you to meet as a group or with your devotional partner to discuss the week. If you are soloing on this journey, the seventh day will be a reflective day for you to solidify what the week has brought into focus. This seven-day format aims to fit easily into a weekly routine.

Why forty days?

The number *forty* has strong symbolism in the Scripture. Forty is a number associated with cleansing, purifying, and preparation. It is especially appropriate for our topic: finding rest in the Promised One. The nation of Israel spent forty years in the desert before they could enter Canaan. During that forty years, God led them, cared for them, protected them, provided for them, and taught them. He was their gentle Father, holding their hand, leading them step-by-step and day by day. He corrected them, refined them, and brought them to mature faith.

Will you make this commitment to forty days of opening your life fully to the Father? Will you consecrate forty days and declare them sacred? Will you commit to schedule a Sabbath Pause every day for forty days?

In making this commitment, don't fall into the trap of legalism. If you miss a day, please don't decide you've failed. Pick up where you left off and move forward. Let these forty days be days of delighting in the Lord, celebrating His finished work. Don't make them into days of drudgery and duty.

A daily plan

1. Write down the beginning and ending days of your forty-day commitment. Log them in your journal and/or on your calendar.

2. Decide what time of day you will schedule your Sabbath Pause and how much time you will commit to it each day.

3. Think through how your times of daily sabbath will be structured. This structure will serve as a starting place. Each day, your time of sabbathing may flow differently. Thinking through a basic structure ensures you will not waste any time deciding what to do. I propose the following structure as a springboard:

> **A. Delight:** Begin your "sabbathing" by focusing your heart and your thoughts on the joyful, loving relationship you have with God—God the Father, God the Son, and God the Spirit. It is to be an exuberant, passionate relationship. He delights in you and so, delight in Him.

> > I delight greatly in the LORD;
> > > my soul rejoices in my God.
> > For he has clothed me with garments of salvation
> > > and arrayed me in a robe of righteousness.
> > (Isa. 61:10a)

> > "He will take great delight in you,
> > > he will quiet you with his love,
> > > he will rejoice over you with singing." (Zeph. 3:17)

> You might want to write these two verses out and keep them with you day and night. They summarize the theme of this forty-day journey: Your delight is in Him and His delight is in you. Sabbath is a sign between you of that delight.

If you are not experiencing that delight in Him, make a decision that you will not let your emotions rule you. Deliberately fasten your mind on Him, and He will awaken joy in you. His delight in you will cause you to delight in Him.

B. Discover: Use these daily meditations as a tool to lead you in making new discoveries about Jesus. "Learn from me," Jesus said. You will never finish learning from Him. Every day new discoveries await the heart that seeks Him. ""Call to me and I will answer you and tell you great and unsearchable things you do not know""" (Jer. 33:3). The Hebrew word translated "tell you" means "to clearly announce, to explain." As you refresh yourself in His presence, seeking Him and calling to Him, He will announce and explain to you things that were previously hidden from you. You will make new discoveries from His Word because He is leading you into all truth and revealing to you the deep things of God. You will learn from Him as He speaks His word directly and personally to you.

C. Distill: As you end your Sabbath Pause, take the time to distill the essence of what God has spoken to you. Learn to let Him clarify His specific message for you each day. You can count on the fact that God sends His living, active Word into your life and that He has given it an assignment. His Word will fulfill its assignment in you.

> "As the rain and the snow
> come down from heaven,
> and do not return to it
> without watering the earth
> and making it bud and flourish,
> so that it yields seed for the sower and bread for the
> eater,
> so is my word that goes out from my mouth:
> It will not return to me empty,

but will accomplish what I desire
and achieve the purpose for which I sent it."
(Isa. 55:10–11)

When the rain and snow descend, the earth extracts from it life-giving moisture and minerals. Following this distillation, it is drawn back toward the sun in the form of vapor. Your thirsty spirit will extract the life-giving essence of God's Word for you. You will distill from it the message He assigned to your heart.

4. Take your sabbath into your day. Your goal is to live in a soul-sabbath.

Meditations and terminology

These daily meditations will lead you on a journey guided by the Lord's Prayer. Each phrase in Jesus' prayer outline is saturated and dripping with wisdom for how to live in a settled peace.

This outline, the Lord's Prayer, is a portion of Jesus' expanded teachings on prayer. For each topic He outlined, He developed the concept further through parables. Most importantly, He put into practice and lived out each phrase. By His life, He taught prayer. Prayer to Him was not a set of words sandwiched between "Our Father" and "Amen." Prayer was the dynamic of His daily living. The settled peace in which He lived had its roots in His ongoing prayer relationship with His Father. As we examine the Lord's Prayer in that light, we will uncover the secret to living in a soul-sabbath.

In the course of these forty days, I refer to certain terms over and over. To ensure that these ideas and terms are clear, let me define them.

Flesh

Occasionally I will use the word *flesh*. I use the term to identify those habits, thought patterns, emotional responses, and ideas that have their roots in your human nature rather than in Christ. *Flesh* refers to those places in your inner being not yet yielded to and filled with His life.

Sabbath

The word *sabbath* in this journey is not a day of the week or a ritual observance. That's why I don't capitalize it. It describes the state your soul can experience—a state in which you are at rest because of the finished work of God. Often I will use it as a verb, meaning, "Relax; be at peace; let go." The Hebrew word is *shabath.*

Peace

Our English word *peace* does not capture the full meaning of the Hebrew word for peace, *shalom. Shalom* means "total well-being." It means "to be complete or whole." It refers to mental, spiritual, emotional, physical, and even financial well-being. It also means that you are at peace with others and at peace with yourself. When I use the word *peace,* I am referring to the *shalom* kind of peace.

Rest

The Hebrew word is *menuha.* It means more than absence of activity. It means "settled and stable." The word is used, for example, to describe Solomon. He was a man of rest *(menuha),* and the Lord promised to give him rest from his enemies (1 Chron. 22:9).

It's also used to describe the concept of being at home or settling in. God calls the Temple the place of His *menuha.* David said, "'I had it in my heart to build a house as a place of rest *[menuha]* for the ark of the covenant of the LORD, for the footstool of our God, and I made plans to build it'" (1 Chron. 28:2). God asks in Isaiah 66:1: "Where is the house you will build for me? / Where will my resting place *[menuha]* be?"

Are you getting the picture? *Menuha* kind of rest is a stable, established, composed, quiet, still, tranquil soul.

David wrote in Psalm 23: "He leads me beside still waters." The sentence says, "He leads me beside the waters of *menuha.*" Waters of rest. This *menuha* kind of rest is not an absence of movement. Water, by its very nature, cannot be "still" in that sense. Rather, it means calm and gentle, not rushing and forceful. David says that the shepherd leads us "beside" or "alongside," which suggests the path of a stream—water that is moving, but moving gently. The sound of gently flowing water is universally experienced as a peaceful, tranquil, restful sound. Something about it soothes. The path along which He leads you will always be beside the waters of rest. Learn to attune your spiritual ears to always hear the sound of still waters.

SECTION 2
FORTY DAYS

*To pray is nothing more involved than to let Jesus
into our needs. . . . To pray is nothing more involved than
to open the door, giving Jesus access to our needs and permitting
Him to exercise His own power in dealing with them.*
— O. Hallesby, *Prayer*

WEEK 1

Hallowed Be Your Name

" 'Our Father in heaven,
hallowed be your name.' "
(Matt. 6:9)

As His life in you molds you, forms you into His image from one degree of glory to the next, He is fashioning a heart that desires the Father's glory. Underneath all your swirling emotions and the pull of your human nature is the Spirit of the Son, sent into your heart, crying, *"Abba,* Father! Glorify Your name!"

~ Day 1 ~

Delight Yourself in Him

"'O Lord, let your ear be attentive to the prayer of this your servant and to the prayer of your servants who delight in revering your name'" (Neh. 1:11). Take time to take pleasure in His name. You are sabbathing in His arms. It is a sign between you of the delight you take in one another.

Discover

"'Our Father in heaven,
hallowed be your name.'"
(Matt. 6:9)

When I was expecting my first child, it occurred to me that I would have a new name, a name I had never been called before. For the first time, someone would call me Mommy. Even though billions of women have the same name, the name Mommy would still be entirely unique and my own because it named the relationship between me and my child. Even though billions of women are Mommy to someone, only I would be Mommy to Brantley Quin Dean.

As I considered this monumental change in my life, I began to worry: How will my child learn my name? Since no one else calls me Mommy, how will he know to?

I reached this conclusion: I'll tell him my name. I'll weave it into his life, identifying it with his experience of me. As we interact; as we bond; as we come to know each other, I'll teach him my name. That's the only way Brantley Quin Dean will know my name.

Of course, Mommy is not my legal name. Mommy is only my name to my children. It would be silly for anyone else to call me Mommy, because I'm only Mommy to Brantley, Kennedy, and Stinson. To them, that's my name—because to them, that's our relationship. When they were little and we were in a place with other little children, sometimes I would hear the cry, "Mommy!" I would look around to see who said it. If my child didn't call it, then it was not my name being called. Mommy is the name that defines *my* role in *my* children's lives.

In the same way, God has carefully and patiently taught us His name—the name that defines the relationship, the name that explains the bond. He introduced Himself to Moses. "Whom shall I tell them sent me?" Moses asked the Voice from the burning bush. "Tell them I AM has sent you," the Voice answered (see Exod. 3:13–14).

In this way, God began to teach His children His name. God's name is too big, His investment in us too far-reaching, His love for us too boundless to be packaged in one word. So first He gave an open-ended name: I AM. He left room for our understanding of Him and of our relationship to Him to expand. He grows our knowledge of His name with each encounter. He weaves it into our experience of Him. We continue to learn new parts of His name as we continue to learn new truths about His ways. Each new piece of His name that He teaches us introduces us to a new aspect of our relationship to Him. "This is Who I am to you," He is saying. "This is what our relationship entitles you to call Me."

The Father wants you to know His name. He wants you to know that you have a relationship with Him that gives you unique access to Him; that binds you to Him with an unbreakable bond. As you let this truth take hold of you, you will find yourself filled with peace and complete well-being. *Shalom* will define your days.

- What does the word *Father* mean to you? Your response to the word may be positive or negative, depending on your own experience. Very likely, you will have a mixed response. Write out your thoughts honestly.

_____

_____

_____

• What do you want the name Father to mean to you?

_____

_____

_____

• Will you ask your heavenly Father to teach you His name? Write out your thoughts to Him.

_____

_____

_____

Distill

Quiet your thoughts. Turn your ear toward Him. What is the primary thing He has said to you? Trust what you hear Him say to you. Write it down.

_____

_____

_____

~ Day 2 ~

Delight Yourself in Him

"'Then the Almighty will be your gold, / the choicest silver for you. / Surely then you will find delight in the Almighty / and will lift up your face to God'" (Job 22:25–26). Ask the Lord to clear your heart of anything that is not Him. Ask Him to make Himself your treasure and your delight, just as He considers you His treasure: "'They will be mine,' says the LORD Almighty, 'in the day when I make up my treasured possession'" (Mal. 3:17).

Discover

God sent the Spirit of his Son into our hearts,
the Spirit who calls out, "Abba, Father."
(Gal. 4:6)

Jesus brought the Father into clear focus. He magnified the Lord. When you put something invisible to the naked eye on a slide and put it under a microscope, the invisible becomes visible. Not only is it visible, but it is magnified so that the details are clear and discernable. What was hidden is revealed. This is what Jesus did in His earthly form. "No one has ever seen God, but God the One and Only, who is at the Father's side, has made him known" (John 1:18).

One of the most surprising truths that Jesus revealed about God is that we can call Him Father. This offended the religious leaders of His day. "For this reason the Jews tried all the harder to kill him; not only was he breaking the Sabbath, but he was even calling God his own Father, making himself equal with God" (John 5:18). That made God too accessible.

The idea of God as Father was not absent from Jewish thinking. The Old Testament is sprinkled with hints of His father-relationship with His people. But Jesus made it intensely personal.

He took this thought (God as Father) that had been a stray guest, hovering uncertainly on the dim borderland and circumference of men's minds, and *made it the center of everything.* Before Jesus many good people had thought of God's relationship to men mainly in terms of a potter and his clay, or a creator and his creatures, or a dictator and his subjects. But to Jesus all these conceptions were dim half-lights, hiding as much as they revealed. . . . Now that new emphasis of Jesus, that centralization of this conception, was something unheard of and revolutionary; and it changed the whole face of religion.[5]

At the moment of His greatest emotional agony, Jesus called out, *"Abba,* Father" (Mark 14:36)! As He faced the cross and all its suffering; as He stood poised to take upon Himself the sins of the world; as He wrestled with His dread, He cried, *"Abba,* Father."

Abba is the Aramaic word that means "daddy" or "papa." It is the form of intimate address. At this moment of raw emotion in Jesus' life, when the Gospels record that some of His private praying was in the disciples' hearing, Jesus called out, "Daddy!" It makes me think that in all those hours He spent alone with God, outside anyone's hearing, Jesus also called God "Daddy." The Scripture tells us that when Jesus indwells us, He still calls out, *"Abba,* Father"—"Daddy."

Let Him teach you today that God's name to you, His beloved child, is Daddy. You are allowed to address Him intimately, with spontaneous love. He wants you to experience a relationship with Him that is comfortable; close; cozy. Because you know Him as Daddy, you can be confident that anything that concerns you is important to Him. He dotes on you. You are the apple of His eye. You can count on Him.

Oswald Chambers wrote in his book *Christian Disciplines*:

A dear little friend of mine, not four years old, facing one day some big difficulty to her little heart, with a very wise shake of her head, said, "I'll go and tell my papa." Presently she came back, this time with every fiber of her little body strutting with the pride that shone in her eye, "Now my papa's coming!" Presently her papa came, she clasped her little hands and screamed with delight, and danced round about him, unspeakably confident in her papa. Child of God, does something face you that terrifies your heart? Say, "I'll tell my Father." Then come back boasting in the Lord, "Now my Father's coming." And when He comes, you too will clasp your hands in rapture, your mouth will be filled with laughter, and you will be like one that dreams.[6]

My dear friend, He will never let you down. He will never neglect you or withhold good from you. He has settled His love on you and His love for you does not change. His heart is set on you to do you good.

"Though the mountains be shaken
   and the hills be removed,
yet my unfailing love for you will not be shaken
   nor my covenant of peace be removed,"
   says the LORD, who has compassion on you. (Isa. 54:10)

He is your Daddy, your Papa. Rest in His presence. Be confident in His love for you.

- Right now, practice calling God "Daddy." Don't think you are being irreverent. He is King of Kings and Lord of Lords, Creator and Ruler of the universe, Most High God, worthy of all honor and praise . . . and, He is your Daddy.
- Write to Him about what is bothering you or worrying you right now. What is robbing you of peace? Tell Him all about it. At the end, write, "Now my papa's coming!"

_____

_____

Distill

Quiet your thoughts. Turn your ear toward Him. What is the primary thing He has said to you? Trust what you hear Him say to you. Write it down.

_____

_____

_____

~ *Day 3* ~

Delight Yourself in Him

"My tongue will speak of your righteousness / and of your praises all day long" (Ps. 35:28). Delight in His character. Celebrate His trustworthiness. Let Him remind you of His steadfast love for you. Put your love for Him into words; speak your words of love to Him. Feel His pleasure.

Discover

"For the pagan world runs after all such things,
and your Father knows that you need them."
(Luke 12:30)

Your relationship to God as Father can be the basis for restful living. Consider who your Father is.

The fact that God is your Father is not just a lovely idea or a comforting thought. It has day-by-day, minute-by-minute practical effect in your life. He is your provider. He's going to take care of you. He knows what you need and has already made arrangements to provide it.

"Consider how the lilies grow. They do not labor or spin. Yet I tell you, not even Solomon in all his splendor was dressed like one of these. If that is how God clothes the grass of the field, which is here today, and tomorrow is thrown into the fire, how much more will he clothe you, O you of little faith! And do not set your heart on what you will eat or drink; do not worry about it. For the pagan world runs after all such things, and your Father knows that you need them. But seek his kingdom, and these things will be given to you as well.

"Do not be afraid, little flock, for your Father has been pleased
to give you the kingdom." (Luke 12:27–32)

Jesus contrasted three things: the lilies, the pagans (those who do
not know God as Father), and those to whom God is Father. First, consider how the lilies grow. Effortlessly. Without strain or anxiety. They
simply receive their provision. Then He pointed to those who do not
know God. In contrast to the lily, they run after, crave, search diligently
for, and use all their energy making provision for themselves. Finally, He
referred to those to whom God is Father. You need not expend emotional
and spiritual energy acquiring those things your Father already knows
you need. Freed from anxiety about your daily needs, you can run after,
crave, search diligently for, and use your energy to discover the kingdom
of God.

When your mind and your emotions are at rest, you energetically
act out your obedience to Him. When your soul is sabbathing, your
response to His voice is uninhibited. Whatever noises and demands may
fall on your physical ears, your spiritual ears hear the continual soothing
sound of the waters of rest, still waters. Wherever He leads you in the
world, He leads your soul beside still waters.

- Is there a need in your life right now for which you cannot see provision? Write it down.

_____

_____

- Will you surrender that need to your Father and invite Him to use
  this need as the platform for His power? Write down your surrender.

_____

_____

• Now sit beside the still waters. He who has ears to hear, let him hear.

Distill

Quiet your thoughts. Turn your ear toward Him. What is the primary thing He has said to you? Trust what you hear Him say to you. Write it down.

_____

_____

_____

~ Day 4 ~

Delight Yourself in Him

"The Sovereign LORD is my strength; / he makes my feet like the feet of a deer, / he enables me to go on the heights" (Hab. 3:19). Do you want to climb to the heights? Rest in His strength. Let His strength flow through you and be yours. Because of His life in you, you can navigate the heights with agility and surefooted finesse.

Discover

Yet, O Lord, you are our Father.
We are the clay, you are the potter;
we are all the work of your hand.
(Isa. 64:8)

In the Hebraic mind, the concept of God's fatherhood was tied to the creation account. As God created the earth and established life upon it, He pronounced that each species would bring forth its own kind.

> And God said, "Let the land produce living creatures according to their kinds: livestock, creatures that move along the ground, and wild animals, each according to its kind." And it was so. God made the wild animals according to their kinds, the livestock according to their kinds, and all the creatures that move along the ground according to their kinds. And God saw that it was good.
> Then God said, "Let us make man in our image, in our likeness. . . ."
> So God created man in his own image,
> in the image of God he created him;
> male and female he created them. (Gen. 1:24–27)

One aspect of the father-child relationship, then, was that humans, in the beginning, were "fathered" by God. Humankind was made in His image or after His kind. Later, the Lord intensified His relationship with Israel by singling them out, forming a nation that was uniquely His own. Through Abraham and Sarah, He fathered a nation and established a people who would display His glory, as a child displays the characteristics of the father. Through the prophet Isaiah, He described His people as "everyone who is called by my name, / whom I created for my glory, / whom I formed and made" (Isa. 43:7).

Since Jehovah "formed and made" them; since they were His creation and His expression of Himself, they were as clay in His hands. They were a work in progress. Their Father was also their designer. He alone could mold them into His image. These two images, father and potter, were not incompatible: a father's responsibility is to help mold and shape the character of his children. Children can be an expression of the father both genetically and in character.

Jesus, in teaching us to call God "Father," had these concepts in mind. You have been born again. God is your Father.

> To all who received him, to those who believed in his name, he gave the right to become children of God—children born not of natural descent, nor of human decision or a husband's will, but born of God. (John 1:12–13)
>
> For you have been born again, not of perishable seed, but of imperishable. (1 Pet. 1:23)
>
> No one who is born of God will continue to sin, because God's seed remains in him; he cannot go on sinning, because he has been born of God. (1 John 3:9)

God as your Father literally means that His life is in you. He has breathed into you His breath. Just as God breathed His life into Adam at creation, so at rebirth, Jesus breathed on His disciples. "He breathed on them and said, 'Receive the Holy Spirit'" (John 20:22). When the Holy

Spirit came at Pentecost to fill all believers, His coming sounded like a rushing wind. "Suddenly a sound like the blowing of a violent wind came from heaven and filled the whole house where they were sitting" (Acts 2:2). In both the Greek and Hebrew languages, the word for "spirit," "wind," and "breath" is the same. In Greek the word is *pneuma;* in Hebrew the word is *ruach.* It is fully in line with the Scripture to believe that what sounded like a mighty wind was the very breath of Jesus, breathing His life into His followers. At your rebirth, He breathed His life into you too.

Now your Father is forming you into the image of His Son, who is the image of God. He is molding you from the inside out. You are a work in progress.

> *Work of My Hands, I know that sometimes My sculpting hurts. Sometimes you feel as though you are looking less like Me rather than more like Me. Don't worry. It's just a stage in the sculpting process. There are intervals in the work of precisely shaping you during which you look like a shapeless, formless lump of clay. Your old shape has been destroyed, but your new shape has not yet emerged. Don't give up. I am the Master Artist. Those are My hands you feel squeezing you and pushing you. I know exactly what I'm doing. . . .*
>
> *. . . Blessed One, part of the shaping is done by fire. But it is not a destroying fire; it is a cleansing fire. When you walk through it, it will not burn you. It will refine you. I am in the fire. It is going to burn away the earth stuff still clinging to you. It is going to set the work I have finished so the shape is stable.*[7]

- What part of your character do you feel God is sculpting? What circumstances is He using to do His shaping?

  _____

  _____

  _____

• Can you thank your Father for loving you enough to personally shape and mold you into a masterpiece of His design? Choose to thank Him for the circumstances that are forming you into His image. Write out your thanks to Him, specifically naming those circumstances.

_____

_____

_____

Distill

Quiet your thoughts. Turn your ear toward Him. What is the primary thing He has said to you? Trust what you hear Him say to you. Write it down.

_____

_____

_____

~ *Day 5* ~

Delight Yourself in Him

"'Arise, shine, for your light has come, / and the glory of the LORD rises upon you. . . . The LORD rises upon you / and his glory appears over you'" (Isa. 60:1–2). Enjoy His presence. His glory is shining on you, and you are reflecting His glory, just like the moon reflects the sun's light. What joy He takes in you! What pleasure you bring Him! Be quiet and absorb His love. Reflect it today to everyone with whom you come in contact.

Discover

"Father, glorify your name!"
(John 12:28)

The time for His crucifixion drew near. Jesus, in His humanness, struggled with the ordeal He was facing. He said to His disciples, "'Now my heart is troubled, and what shall I say? "Father, save me from this hour?" No, it was for this very reason I came to this hour. Father, glorify your name!'" (John 12:27–28).

His human nature longed for an easier way. But His struggle was put to rest as He subjugated His emotions to the purpose of the Father. Beyond the emotion was the will. At His core, He willed the Father to glorify His name, and His emotions did not rule His actions.

When Jesus first responded to His disciples' request, "Lord, teach us to pray," His circumstances were not as intense. The cross was not yet looming, only hours away. In that quieter, less volatile moment, He taught them, "Pray like this: Father, hallow Your name" (my paraphrase). When His circumstances pressed in on Him, bringing out what was really inside, His heart's cry was still, "Father, glorify Your name!" When He, the Prayer Teacher, teaches you and me to pray, "Father, hallow Your name," it is not just a meaningless or rote recitation. He did not just teach it. He lived it.

As His life in you molds you, forms you into His image from one degree of glory to the next, He is fashioning a heart that desires the Father's glory. Underneath all your swirling emotions and the pull of your human nature is the Spirit of the Son, sent into your heart, crying, *"Abba, Father! Glorify Your name!"* Your will can win out over your emotions. You will find a settled peace as you surrender to your true heart's cry: "Father, glorify Your name. Whatever path it sets me on; whatever 'flesh' must go to the cross; Father, glorify Your name!"

• What is your struggle right now? What has your emotions in turmoil?

_____

_____

_____

• Draw on what you know of the Father. What do you think His purpose is? What higher good is being worked out?

_____

_____

_____

• Will you let your will be aligned with His purpose? Can you say, "For this very reason I came to this hour"? Write your thoughts. It will help you solidify them.

_____

_____

_____

- Write out this prayer. Make it yours: *Father, glorify Your name.*

_____

_____

_____

Distill

Quiet your thoughts. Turn your ear toward Him. What is the primary thing He has said to you? Trust what you hear Him say to you. Write it down.

_____

_____

_____

~ Day 6 ~

Review and Reflect

- How do you feel about calling God "Daddy"?

  _____

  _____

  _____

- What does it mean to you that He has initiated and invited such intimacy?

  _____

  _____

  _____

- In your specific, personal circumstances right now, what difference does it make that God is your Daddy?

  _____

  _____

  _____

- What does this verse mean to you today?

  God sent the Spirit of his Son into our hearts, the Spirit who calls out, "Abba, Father." (Gal. 4:6)

  _____

  _____

  _____

~ Day 7 ~

Journal Your Thoughts and Prayers

_____

_____

_____

_____

_____

_____

_____

_____

_____

_____

_____

_____

_____

_____

_____

_____

_____

_____

_____

_____

_____

_____

WEEK 2

Your Will Be Done

"'Your kingdom come,
your will be done
on earth as it is in heaven.'"
(Matt. 6:10)

His will in every situation will lead to restoration, healing, and wholeness. You can trust that His plan will reflect His love for you. You can find soul-rest in knowing that His desire for you and for those you love is to prosper you and not to harm you; to give you a hope and a future.

~ Day 8 ~

Delight Yourself in Him

"My soul finds rest in God alone; / my salvation comes from him" (Ps. 62:1). Rest in the fact that He is the source of a perpetual, never-ending deliverance. In everything that comes into your life, He is actively and aggressively acting on your behalf. You are safe. In Him, you can find rest for your soul. He is leading you beside still waters.

Discover

"'Your kingdom come,
your will be done
on earth as it is in heaven.'"
(Matt. 6:10)

With these few words, the Prayer Teacher showed us an astounding truth about the role of prayer. Prayer is the conduit that brings the direct, intervening, specific power and provision of God into the circumstances of earth. If all that God has available for earth will be manifested apart from prayer, then why would Jesus include this petition in His pattern for prayer?

This is not an arm's-length, passive prayer. Rather, it is an assertive, proactive prayer. In section 1, you looked at the fact that God's work is finished but that finished work must come from the spiritual realm (heaven) to the material realm (earth). Prayer is how the will of God that is finished in heaven comes into the circumstances of earth. Prayer releases the power of God to accomplish the purposes of God.

Jesus is not teaching us to pray some generic, blanket prayer, but instead He wants us to use this prayer in every specific, minute detail of our lives. We can pray, "In this detail, Father, let Your finished work be expressed. In this situation, on this day, at this time let Your sovereign rule take direct effect. For this need, let everything available in heaven be manifested on the earth."

Jesus used strong language here. He did not hope or wish God's will would be done, but He declared that God's will be done. When, through prayer, God's people access the power and the plan of God, they can be confident that God's intervening power will take effect and His specific plan will be worked out. The working out of His plan may take a course that at times looks backward, but you can rest assured that it is always forward. Keep prayer flowing from start to finish.

What peace can be yours when you recognize the tool God has put at your disposal! God's work is finished and prayer will bring it into your circumstances. Soul-sabbath means resting in His finished work, and trusting His word that prayer will cause His plan to take effect.

- What is a circumstance in your life right now? It doesn't need to be especially traumatic or difficult; just something in which you want the power and provision of God to be manifested. Let the Spirit of God surface in your thoughts what situation or circumstance to consider.

  _____

  _____

  _____

- List details of that circumstance. Write down even the smallest, most insignificant details.

  _____

  _____

  _____

- Over each detail, claim the sovereign rule of God and the finished work of God. Over everything that comes to your mind about this situation, pray, "Your kingdom come. Your will be done." Then, trustfully rest.

Distill

Quiet your thoughts. Turn your ear toward Him. What is the primary thing He has said to you? Trust what you hear Him say to you. Write it down.

_____

_____

_____

~ Day 9 ~

Delight Yourself in Him

"The LORD delights in those who fear him, / who put their hope in his unfailing love" (Ps. 147:11). Let the Lord delight in you. Remember that He put sabbath-rest in place as a sign of His unfailing commitment to you. As you are learning to rest in Him and participate in His sabbath, He is delighting in you.

Discover

Do not conform any longer to the pattern of this world,
but be transformed by the renewing of your mind.
Then you will be able to test and approve
what God's will is—his good, pleasing and perfect will.
(Rom. 12:2)

When you discover the great truth that prayer activates the specific will of God in a situation, the thought will be restful only if you have moved to the place of willing the will of God. Often we can have an underlying sense that God's will is something we have to bear up under or settle for. God's will, we think, is difficult and oppressive.

In Romans 12:2, Paul described God's will with three words: *good, pleasing,* and *perfect.* Greek words used might be translated "beneficial," "bringing pleasure," and "a perfect fit." Only when you come to know God through experience—when you have put His will to the test and have firsthand understanding that it is good—can you find rest and peace in the thought of His will being done. But the secret to experiencing God this way is that you first have to obey Him and surrender to Him in order to put His will to the test. You have to take the one step in front of you. You have to abandon the old familiar flesh-ways.

You have to set your face like flint in the direction He is pointing you, making no provision to turn back. Only then can you say, "Your promises have been thoroughly tested, / and your servant loves them" (Ps. 119:140).

In the Scripture, words involving the senses describe how you will know God. For example, "Taste and see that the LORD is good" (Ps. 34:8); "I pray also that the eyes of your heart may be enlightened" (Eph. 1:18); and "'He who has ears to hear, let him hear'" (Mark 4:9). Why do you think God used sense words? I think it is because those things that you know by your senses, you know because of firsthand experience. Could you, for example, describe the taste of a fresh strawberry to someone who has never tasted a fresh strawberry? Could you describe the sound of rain or the smell of the ocean to a person who has never heard rain or smelled the ocean? What you know by means of your senses, you know because you have experienced it. So it is with the deep things of God. You must first know Him by experience. Then you will know with certainty that His will is good, pleasing, and perfect.

God reveals His will progressively. He unfolds it obedience by obedience. "The path of the righteous is like the first gleam of dawn, / shining ever brighter till the full light of day" (Prov. 4:18). Each obedience sets the stage for the next step. As you keep putting His promises to the test, you will discover that where there used to be hesitancy and uncertainty, there is now a settled confidence. Your steps that started out halting and tentative are now sure and steady. Little by little, step by step, you prove the will of God to be good, pleasing, and perfect.

Once you know for yourself that God's will is desirable, you will be able to trust that His will for all situations is equally desirable. You will learn to pray with expectant joy, "Let Your kingdom come. Let Your will be done. As in heaven, so on earth." You will rest on His will completely.

Upon God's will I lay me down,
　　As child upon its mother's breast;
No silken couch, nor softest bed,
　　Could ever give me such deep rest.

Thy wonderful, grand will, my God,
　　With triumph now I make it mine;
And faith shall cry a joyous Yes!
　　To every dear command of Thine.[8]

- Do you know firsthand that God's will is desirable? Let the Spirit remind you of the times when you learned through experience that His plan exceeds your expectations. List them.

_____

_____

_____

_____

- As you remember, let faith spring up. As you sit quietly by the still waters, let peace flow through your heart. Whatever He is calling you to now, you can trust His plan. Whatever you are praying about, you can trust His will. Write out your thoughts.

_____

_____

_____

_____

Distill

Quiet your thoughts. Turn your ear toward Him. What is the primary thing He has said to you? Trust what you hear Him say to you. Write it down.

_____

_____

_____

~ *Day 10* ~

Delight Yourself in Him

"I guide you in the way of wisdom / and lead you along straight paths. / When you walk, your steps will not be hampered; / when you run, you will not stumble" (Prov. 4:11–12). Entrust yourself to Him. His way is safe and secure. It is the sabbath way—the way of rest and peace. It leads beside the waters of rest.

Discover

"For I have come down from heaven not to do my will
but to do the will of him who sent me."
(John 6:38)

Jesus, while on earth in His physical form, showed us what a life completely abandoned to God's will looked like. His fully surrendered life was a life through which all the power of God flowed freely. His very words tell us that He *chose* the will of God over His human will, time after time. He yielded His will to God's every moment. "'For I have come down from heaven not to do my will but to do the will of him who sent me'" (John 6:38). Because He chose the Father's will, He worked the Father's works. "'It is the Father, living in me, who is doing his work. Believe me when I say that I am in the Father and the Father is in me; or at least believe on the evidence of the miracles themselves'" (John 14:10–11). The Father's miracles flowed onto the earth and into the lives of individuals through Jesus. Jesus' surrender to God's will made it possible for the Father's finished work to be manifested on earth.

Jesus is far more to us than an example. The very life He lived on earth through His human nature He now lives in me and in you. Just as His life while on earth was marked by an absolute surrender to the Father's will, so His life in me forms the same desire in me: not my will, but His will. God is actively and energetically working in you to create desires that match His will. "It is God who works in you to will . . . his good purpose" (Phil. 2:13). Your will is progressively being fused into oneness with His.

In John 17 we read a prayer that Jesus prayed for us. In this prayer, I find it interesting that He referred to two different types of His glory. He spoke first of a glory that belonged to Him before the world began.

> "And now, Father, glorify me in your presence with the glory I
> had with you before the world began." (17:5)

Jesus set aside this glory when He emptied Himself and took upon Himself the form of a man. This glory the Father restored to Him when He returned to the Father's right hand. But He also referred to another kind of glory—a glory that belonged to Him on earth.

> "I have given them the glory that you gave me." (17:22)

One kind of glory was inherently His and had been His throughout eternity; and another glory God gave Him while He lived on the earth, and that is the glory He passed on to His disciples. What was the glory of the *man* Jesus? He was the vessel that contained the Father's life. He was the instrument through which the Father operated. He was one with the Father.

He passed on that glory to His followers. The Father would be in Jesus; Jesus would be in His followers. His followers would be one with Jesus as Jesus is one with the Father. "'I have given them the glory that you gave me, that they may be one as we are one: I in them and you in me'" (John 17:22–23). Jesus, in these thoughts, is not emphasizing unity among believers, but the unity of the believer with Him—which produces unity among believers! The indwelling Christ Himself is our unity.

The glory He has given us is that each of us is a vessel that contains His life; each of us is an instrument through which He operates. His life flows through us and apart from Him we can do nothing. His life in us, our hope of glory.

He is producing in me the complete surrender to the will of the Father that is the hallmark of His life. As He works mightily in me, my heart's desire becomes, "Not my will. Your will. All I want is what You want. Let Your will be done."

- Read John 15:5. Do you really believe that you can do nothing apart from Him? Define what *nothing* means to you in this context.

_____

_____

_____

- What situations, plans, relationships, or desires are you retaining ownership of? What pieces of your life are you resisting full surrender to Him?

_____

_____

_____

_____

- Honestly examine your heart. Why do you resist turning these pieces completely over to His will?

_____

_____

_____

- Stay quiet in His presence until you feel yourself letting go. Adapt the prayer from Mark 9:24: *I do surrender. Help me overcome my "unsurrender!"*

Distill

Quiet your thoughts. Turn your ear toward Him. What is the primary thing He has said to you? Trust what you hear Him say to you. Write it down.

_____

_____

_____

~ Day 11 ~

Delight Yourself in Him

"I trust in your unfailing love; / my heart rejoices in your salvation" (Ps. 13:5). When you have full confidence in His love for you, your heart will be kept in perfect peace. Let your thoughts dwell on His unfailing love and His ongoing salvation. Enjoy a sabbath of the heart.

Discover

"I know the plans I have for you," declares the LORD, "plans to prosper you and not to harm you, plans to give you hope and a future."
(Jer. 29:11)

His will in every situation will lead to restoration, healing, and wholeness. You can trust that His plan will reflect His love for you. You can find soul-rest in knowing that His desire for you and for those you love is to prosper you and not to harm you; to give you a hope and a future. The word translated "prosper" is *shalom,* which is "total well-being of body, soul, and spirit; prosperity and success; completeness." His will is always for your *shalom.*

You will rest in your soul when you are certain that His every thought toward you and His every plan for you is good. "You are good, and what you do is good" (Ps. 119:68). His plan completes you. Surrender yourself fully to His way.

> I remember the turmoil of soul I experienced before committing myself to follow Him on whatever path He would lead— remember as if it were yesterday. But at last—oh, the rest that came to me when I lifted my head and followed! For in acceptance, there lies peace.
> *Amy Carmichael*

There is a way chosen for you. "Who, then, is the man that fears the LORD? / He will instruct him in the way chosen for him" (Ps. 25:12). God has a specific plan for you, and as you trust and follow Him, the plan unfolds. His will for you, His design for your life, fits you in every way. It is not a generic, off-the-rack plan that would fit just anyone. He has designed a life just for you. As you surrender to Him, you do not lose yourself; you find yourself. As you obey Him step by step, a steadfast peace settles on you. Your heart cries, "My food is to do the will of the one who sent me!" His will satisfies your deepest yearnings, nourishes your soul, strengthens you. His will is all you need and all you desire.

> Lord, do what thou pleasest with me and mine. I refer myself to thee, and am well satisfied that all thy counsel concerning me should be performed.
> *Matthew Henry*

> What Thou wilt; as Thou wilt; when Thou wilt.
> *Thomas à Kempis*

Everything that He has planned for you and has promised you, He will perform.

> The LORD will fulfill his purpose for me;
>   your love, O LORD, endures forever—
>   do not abandon the works of your hands. (Ps. 138:8)

When the angel Gabriel visited Mary and announced to her that she would give birth to the long-awaited Messiah, he concluded his conversation: "'For nothing is impossible with God'" (Luke 1:37). The Greek translated exactly says, "No word of God shall be void of power."[9] The phrase employs *rehma* for *word*. *Rehma* means "a word or phrase being spoken in the present by a living voice." In essence, Gabriel tells Mary, "What God is saying to you *will* be accomplished because He never speaks a word that does not have power in it."

Mary responded, "'Behold, the bondslave of the Lord; be it done to me according to your word *[rhema]*'" (Luke 1:38, NASB). Later we read, "'But Mary treasured up all these things *[rhema]*, pondering them in her heart'" (Luke 2:19, NASB).

The Father is speaking to you. He is placing in your heart a sense of expectation. He is creating in your mind a certainty. He is moving your desires and dreams in the direction of His will. Let your response be as Mary's: May it be done to me according to your word.

The Father is able to bring into being everything He promises. You can trust His will because you know Him. He is faithful. He is trustworthy. He is sovereign. He is ruler over heaven and earth. He sees the whole picture. He is bringing about the best possible outcome. He loves you with an unshakeable love.

"'Blessed is [the one] who has believed that what the Lord has said to her [or him] will be accomplished!'" (Luke 1:45).

- Do you believe that the Lord has a plan for you? Do you believe that He created you with a specific purpose in mind? If so, what does that say to you about your value to Him? Write out your thoughts.

  _____

  _____

  _____

- Do you trust that the plan He has for you is good and will ultimately prove to be pleasing to you? If so, will you right now surrender every moment, every thought, and every circumstance to Him for the working out of that plan? Write down specifically what you are surrendering.

  _____

  _____

Distill

Quiet your thoughts. Turn your ear toward Him. What is the primary thing He has said to you? Trust what you hear Him say to you. Write it down.

_____

_____

_____

~ Day 12 ~

Delight Yourself in Him

"I have set the LORD always before me. / Because he is at my right hand, / I will not be shaken. / Therefore my heart is glad and my tongue rejoices; / my body also will rest secure" (Ps. 16:8–9). As your soul comes to rest in Him, even your body will change. Take time to feel the peace in your heart flow through your body. Let the still waters flood your emotions with peace.

Discover

"My Father, if it is possible, may this cup be taken from me.
Yet not as I will, but as you will."
(Matt. 26:39)

In the hours before His arrest, Jesus endured an agony such as no other human being has ever or will ever know. He wrestled with His human emotions and responses. "He began to be sorrowful and troubled. Then he said to them, 'My soul is overwhelmed with sorrow to the point of death'" (Matt. 26:37–38). Sometimes we are faced with a trial about which we have no choice, and so we must reconcile ourselves to it. But in this case, Jesus had a choice. He did not have to endure the cross. He marched into the crucifixion horror by His own free will.

As the moment was upon Him, He cried out to the Father, "Abba, is there any other way for Your plan to be put into effect? Is there any way around this?" (my paraphrase). Three times He prayed along these lines. One of these prayers was: "'My Father, if it is not possible for this cup to be taken away unless I drink it, may your will be done'" (Matt. 26:42). His agonized praying continued long into the night. But when He finished praying, His soul had found such rest in God's will that He could meet what He so dreaded head-on. "'Look, the hour is near, and the Son of Man is betrayed into the hands of sinners. Rise, let us go! Here comes my betrayer!'" (Matt. 26:45–46).

Don't imagine that Jesus walked through His ordeal stoically. All of His humanity was involved. No doubt He screamed in pain when the whip tore His back and the nails ripped His hands and feet. I imagine that the betrayal of trusted friends brought Him to tears. But there was, underneath it all, a settled peace. A supernatural strength and endurance. A certainty. A firmness of purpose. *Shalom, menuha, shabath.*

During His long nighttime struggle, when His emotional anguish became so intense He felt that He could die from it, the core of His prayer remained, "Let Your will be done." As He continued in prayer until His human emotions lined up with God's plan, the Father had the access to Him needed to cement in Jesus' mind and heart the solid reality that carried Him through:

1. I am in control. No one else has power over you or your circumstances. (see John 19:11)
2. This will work out according to My plan that has been in place since before the world began. (see John 12:27; and Acts 2:22–24)
3. You can look forward to the results that I will bring from this. (see Heb. 12:2)
4. Your obedience will give Me the opportunity to glorify Myself. (see John 12:28)

All of this is true for you. You will never come close to Jesus' experience, but the same reality that was the foundation of His peace is also your reality. When you reach the place of truly praying, "Not what I will, but what You will," His *shalom* will undergird you; His *menuha* will give you strength; His *shabath* will carry you through.

- Be still. Take time to let these words penetrate your heart and mind as they relate to your life and situation:

1. I am in control. No one else has power over you or any of your
   circumstances.

   _____

   _____

2. This will work out according to My plan that has been in place since
   before the world began.

   _____

   _____

3. You can look forward to the results that I will bring from this.

   _____

   _____

4. Your obedience will give Me the opportunity to glorify Myself.

   _____

   _____

Distill

Quiet your thoughts. Turn your ear toward Him. What is the primary
thing He has said to you? Trust what you hear Him say to you. Write it
down.

_____

_____

_____

~ Day 13 ~

Review and Reflect

- Why do you think Jesus included the phrase "Your kingdom come, your will be done on earth as it is in heaven" in His prayer outline?

  _____

  _____

  _____

- How will you come to trust that God's will for you and for your every situation is good, pleasing, and perfect?

  _____

  _____

  _____

- What do you need to do right now to put God's will to the test? God invited you to test His promises and His word so that they can be proved true. This is different from testing God. Putting God's will to the test simply means to depend upon them and give God the opportunity to prove them true. "Your promises have been thoroughly tested, and your servant loves them" (Ps. 119:140).

  _____

  _____

  _____

- Describe the peace that enters your heart and mind when you let go and fully surrender.

_____

_____

_____

- What does this verse mean to you?

Do not conform any longer to the pattern of this world, but be transformed by the renewing of your mind. Then you will be able to test and approve what God's will is—his good, pleasing and perfect will. (Rom. 12:2)

_____

_____

_____

~ Day 14 ~

Journal Your Thoughts and Prayers

_____

_____

_____

_____

_____

_____

_____

_____

_____

_____

_____

_____

_____

_____

_____

_____

_____

_____

_____

WEEK 3

Give Us Today

"Give us today our daily bread."
(Matt. 6:11)

As you keep your life open to the flow of His power, He will supply your every need. Ask Him, and He will gladly give you everything you need and fulfill your heart's true desire. He is looking for opportunities to prove His word to you.

~ Day 15 ~

Delight Yourself in Him

"Show me your face, / let me hear your voice; / for your voice is sweet, / and your face is lovely" (Song of Sol. 2:14). The depth of your yearning for Him is but the shadow cast by His yearning for you. Let His love for you surround you. Let your soul breathe it in. Be amazed by His love.

Discover

"'Give us today our daily bread.'"
(Matt. 6:11)

The Father wants to meet your needs. He encourages you to look to Him to supply every need that arises. He takes pleasure in supplying you with everything you need.

Why do you have needs? Why do you need shelter or food? Why do you need emotional connections with other people? Why do you need to feel a sense of purpose?

You have needs because God created you with needs. He could have made you so that your shelter is on your back, as He did the turtle. He could have made you so that you could live a solitary, isolated life. But instead, He made you with needs. The reason is so that your needs could be His entry points. Your needs will point you to His supply.

"Meet today's needs," Jesus taught us to pray. "Whatever arises today, Father, I look to You for provision."

I hear the Father whisper, "Jennifer, nothing will come into your life today for which I have not already put provision in place. Just be alert and watchful. Look to Me first; I will point you to the supply."

What an adventure it is to live this way! How it frees me from anxiety and frustration! I am learning that everything, from the major to the mundane, has been provided for by my Father. As needs arise from day to day, instead of asking, "Father, do something!" I just say, "Father, what have You already done? Where will I discover the answer You have provided? My soul rests in You, waiting patiently for Your salvation."

Please understand, God does not meet every need in the way that seems most convenient to me. If that were my measuring stick, then I would often be frustrated. But if I have given myself to Him as a living offering, then I am open for Him to meet my needs in ways that will further my understanding of Him or will advance His kingdom. You will only live in sabbath when you have aligned yourself with His will, so that your desire is to know Him at deeper and deeper levels. If your motivating force is to get God to perform for you—to see Him bring about your agenda—you will not find this rest for your soul that Jesus offers. Often an inconvenience in my mind puts me in the path of an encounter the Lord has arranged for me. Or, something that throws off my schedule actually provides me with information I needed—sometimes before I know I needed it.

Between writing the previous paragraph and this one, I changed planes in Dallas, Texas. I left home this morning for Albuquerque, New Mexico. While in Dallas, I stopped by a newsstand to buy a bottle of water and, to my horror, discovered that I had left my wallet with all my cash, all my credit cards, and my driver's license in my car in the airport parking lot in Kansas City. I had checked in at the airport this morning using my driver's license as my required photo ID, then parked my car. Somehow I neglected to put my wallet back in my purse. As I was walking through the airport, thinking about how to best express these thoughts, I had been asking the Lord what incident from my life to use to illustrate the principle I am writing about today. As I sat down in the Dallas airport to think through my options about my driver's license dilemma, I sensed the Father, with a chuckle, saying, "Tell this story." I nearly laughed out loud. I'm going to tell you this story as it unfolds.

Here's my situation: When I get to Albuquerque in an hour or so, I have to either rent a car or take a shuttle to my destination. This will be impossible without cash, credit cards, or a driver's license. Don't you think? But that's not all. Tomorrow morning I have to take that same shuttle or drive that rental car (for which I have no resources) back to the airport to board a flight for Phoenix. Photo ID is required to board a flight. I have none.

Already I can see some of the Father's preparation. First, my wonderful-beyond-words associate, Mary Medley, is to meet me in Phoenix tomorrow. She will be flying in from Kansas City. Let me tell you how easy it will be for Mary to find my car with my wallet sitting in it. This morning when I arrived at the airport, I was running late. Because I will be gone for a week, I would usually have parked in a satellite parking lot—a parking lot where thousands of cars—a sea of cars—are parked every day. However, since I was late, I had to park in circle parking right next to the terminal. Of course, this parking lot was full. I drove around it several times. Then I prayed, "Lord, I'm late for my flight. I have no other options. I believe that You have reserved the perfect parking place for me. Show it to me, please." As I drove through again, a car backed out and I took its spot. The spot was on the very end of a parking row, bordering the main drag of the lot, and two rows from the entrance. It was not the most convenient spot for me to get from my car to the terminal, but it is the most convenient spot for Mary to find my car among the hundreds of cars in the parking lot.

I'm praying right now, "Lord, direct me to the provision You have already put in place when I get to Albuquerque." More later.

Later: I remembered that I had written down the account number and expiration date from one of my credit cards in my calendar. The reason I did that is too long a story to tell you, but I hadn't thought about it in months. The shuttle company used that information and sold me a ticket for today and for tomorrow morning. So far, so good. I have one more hurdle. Tomorrow I have to get on my flight to Phoenix without my driver's license for photo ID. I've had a brainstorm. In my briefcase I have a brochure from an event where I am speaking. The brochure has my picture on it with my name under it. It is not official, but maybe it will do. I'll tell you tomorrow.

Tomorrow: It worked. I had to tell my story twice, but here I am on my flight to Phoenix. Once I arrive in Phoenix I will be reunited with my wallet. As I think about the faith-lab God arranged for me, this verse comes to mind: "Then Jesus asked them, 'When I sent you without purse, bag or sandals, did you lack anything?'" (Luke 22:35).

- What needs are in your life today? Begin asking God what provision He has already made. Commit yourself to being alert and responsive to His promptings. Write out your thoughts.

_____

_____

_____

Distill

Quiet your thoughts. Turn your ear toward Him. What is the primary thing He has said to you? Trust what you hear Him say to you. Write it down.

_____

_____

_____

~ Day 16 ~

Delight Yourself in Him

"'I have told you these things, so that in me you may have peace. In this world you will have trouble. But take heart! I have overcome the world'" (John 16:33). The Lord's presence in your life is the reason you can live in soul-sabbath and perfect rest and peace. Celebrate His presence.

Discover

"Ask and it will be given to you. . . . For everyone who asks receives."
(Matt. 7:7–8)

Jesus used a very simple form of the word *ask* in this declaration. It is worded like a child asking his or her parent to meet a need. Yet Jesus also said, "Your Father knows what you need before you ask him" (Matt. 6:8). If that's so, why ask?

Let me back up a little. The phrase the Father gave me many years ago to define my message is *the praying life.* Don't settle for "having a prayer life"—like you have a home life, and a work life, and a leisure life. Don't be satisfied with a part of your life that is set aside for prayer. Instead, "live a praying life"—a life through which prayer flows unceasingly. A praying life is a life always in active and intentional cooperation with God; a life in which an undercurrent of prayer is always present; a life of continual interaction with the spiritual realm. A praying life is a life open to the power and provision of God. A praying life focuses on, "How do I keep my life open to the Father's power?" One of the ways that you open your life to what God wants to provide is by asking!

In asking, you acknowledge the Source of everything. "Don't be deceived, my dear brothers. Every good and perfect gift is from above, coming down from the Father of the heavenly lights, who does not change like shifting shadows" (James 1:16–17). God instructs you to ask for what you need because this interaction keeps you aware that He is your source.

Another reason God set it up so that your asking releases His supply is because He wants you to see His power. If His method for meeting your needs did not engage you, you would not see His power at work. He wants you to have observable proof of His involvement in your life; He wants you to see His love for you. When you live in an "ask and receive" mode, you cannot help but be aware—and awed by—the Father's intimate involvement in your life.

Sometimes God waits for you to ask because until you see your need, you will not recognize His supply. He waits until you have come to the end of your own resources. He waits for you to turn to Him as the one and only Source.

- What do you need to ask the Lord for? Ask Him now.

_____

_____

_____

- The Lord tells us over and over again to remember: Remember what He has done in the past; remember when He has previously provided. Right now, remember. Recall times when God met your need. Consider that His provision not only met your immediate need; it also provided a foothold for your faith. Let His past action provide confidence for the present. Write down what you remember.

_____

_____

_____

Distill

Quiet your thoughts. Turn your ear toward Him. What is the primary thing He has said to you? Trust what you hear Him say to you. Write it down.

_____

_____

_____

~ Day 17 ~

Delight Yourself in Him

"I said to the LORD, 'You are my Lord; / apart from you I have no good thing'" (Ps. 16:2). Is He everything to you? Spend time praising Him, thanking Him, worshiping Him.

Discover

You do not have, because you do not ask God.
(James 4:2)

Once again we see that our asking releases God's provision. Not asking results in not having. Let's look at the surrounding verses:

> What causes fights and quarrels among you? Don't they come from your desires that battle within you? You want something but don't get it. You kill and covet, but you cannot have what you want. You quarrel and fight. You do not have, because you do not ask God. When you ask, you do not receive, because you ask with wrong motives, that you may spend what you get on your pleasures. (James 4:1–3)

Here is my paraphrase of what James said:

> The battle that rages within you, brought on by your intense desire for what you don't have, spills over into your relationships with others. In trying to get your needs met and your desires fulfilled, you look to other people. But other people can't meet the need, so you end up quarreling and fighting. The answer is simple. Instead of looking to other people for those things you desire, ask God! Now, I know that sometimes

you do ask God and still don't receive. This is because you are asking for something that will bring you more frustration rather than truly meet your need.

"When you ask, you do not receive, because you ask with wrong motives, that you may spend what you get on your pleasures" (James 4:3). Does that mean God does not want to give you anything that is for your pleasure? Does it mean that He is always weighing our motives and if there is any hint of our delight in them, God will withhold? Not at all. God loves to delight you. But He will withhold what you ask for when it would further your weakness rather than bringing you deeper into relationship with Him.

My friend illustrated this kind of love in a conversation recently. She has a daughter whom she loves, who is currently living a rebellious and self-destructive lifestyle. My friend told me how her daughter asked for money and she refused to give it. Her refusal came not because she wanted to withhold money from her daughter. In fact, it was difficult for her to refuse. Her refusal came because she knew that the money would be spent in ways that would harm her daughter. Out of her love for her daughter she refused her daughter's request.

So it is with God. He knows what will keep you from your true destiny and lead you away from His path for you. Sometimes the things we ask for may seem good, even spiritual, but God knows how they will really affect us. For example, imagine that a person asks God for more fruit in ministry, but God seems to withhold it. Could it be that God knows that, at this point in her development, more tangible "success" in her ministry would cause her to be filled with pride? God has some flesh-issues to deal with before He gives more fruit in ministry. Or, suppose a single person asks God for a mate and God seems to withhold the answer. Could it be that God knows that right now a mate would distract the person from his or her wholehearted pursuit of Him? God knows what He is doing, and you can trust Him. You can trust that His motivation is your best interest.

I love to say yes to my children. I love to give them what they ask for. In fact, there are only two reasons I will ever say no. One is if I don't have the resources. The other is if I think it will not ultimately be in their best interest. God loves to say yes to us. He is never short of resources, so the only reason He might not give us exactly what we ask for is because He knows it would not be in our best interest. It would not bring into our lives what we probably think it would bring.

Rest comes in trusting His love for you and His wisdom. Peace is yours when you know that He will never withhold from you something that would truly make your life more complete. When you are living in a flow of prayer—a praying life—you can always know: "God will meet my need in the right way at the right time with the right resources. If it is best for my need to be fully met today, then it will be."

- Is there a need or needs in your life that you are looking to others to meet and not to God? If so, it is causing a battle within you that may be spilling out in fights and quarrels with others. Put this question before God and respond to what He brings to your mind. Write it down.

  _____

  _____

  _____

- Now, ask God for what you need. State your trust in Him to supply your need(s) in the right time and in the right way.

  _____

  _____

  _____

Distill

Quiet your thoughts. Turn your ear toward Him. What is the primary thing He has said to you? Trust what you hear Him say to you. Write it down.

_____

_____

_____

~ Day 18 ~

Delight Yourself in Him

"All my longings lie open before you, O LORD; / my sighing is not hidden from you" (Ps. 38:9). Even the needs and longings you cannot articulate are clear to Him. Rest in the fact that He is meeting needs that are nothing but inner groanings. The groanings that are too deep for words are clear to Him.

Discover

He who did not spare his own Son,
but gave him up for us all—how will he not also,
along with him, graciously give us all things?
(Rom. 8:32)

I think that when Paul wrote this, he echoed words from the Old Testament: "'because you have not withheld from me your son, your only son'" (Gen. 22:12). The context of these words was that God had called upon Abraham to take his only son Isaac, whom he loved, and offer him as a burnt offering. One of the layers of this story is the illustration of what the crucifixion cost the Father.

Abraham, by his radical and unrestrained obedience and trust, put on display his love for Jehovah. Once God had placed him in a position to offer his son Isaac—his only son whom he loved—in utter faith, no more proof was necessary. If Abraham loved God so much that he would not spare his own son, but offer him up in obedience to God, then clearly there was nothing Abraham would withhold from God.

Do you see the picture? If God loves you so much that He would not withhold His Son—His only Son whom He loves—is there anything that He would withhold? Will He not also graciously give you all things?

Do you want proof of how much the Father loves you? Look at the cross.

I have three sons. There are many people for whom I would give my own life, but there is no one for whom I would give my sons' lives. Their lives are far more precious to me than my own. The Father gave His own Son for you. The love He has for you is beyond your scope; beyond your ability to grasp. He withholds nothing from you.

Not only has He given you His Son on the cross—His death in place of yours—He has also given you His Son to live in you—His life in place of yours.

> I no longer live, but Christ lives in me. (Gal. 2:20)
>
> But if Christ is in you . . . (Rom. 8:10)
>
> And if the Spirit of him who raised Jesus from the dead is living in you . . . (Rom 8:11)
>
> . . . Christ in you, the hope of glory. (Col. 1:27)
>
> "I am in you." (John 14:20)

He has given you His Son, not only to die for you, but also to live in you. Would He then withhold anything else? If you feel that God is withholding something from you, you are misreading your situation. Let Him help you redefine it.

The parable of the prodigal son is, among other things, Jesus' story of the Father's provision. The father's display of lavish love as he welcomed home the prodigal son is stunning. My heart is captured, though, by the words he spoke to the elder son:

> "'My son,' the father said, 'you are always with me, and everything I have is yours.'" (Luke 15:31)

Did you catch that? "Everything I have is yours." Anytime the elder brother wanted a robe on his shoulders or a ring on his finger or sandals on his feet; anytime he wanted a celebration with a fattened calf, he could have had it all along. He just never asked.

Everything the Father has is yours. "All things are yours, whether Paul or Apollos or Cephas or the world or life or death or the present or the future—all are yours, and you are of Christ, and Christ is of God" (1 Cor. 3:21–23). Just ask.

- Is there anything you think that God is withholding from you?

  _____

  _____

  _____

- Will you ask Him to help you see the situation from His perspective? What is He showing you?

  _____

  _____

  _____

Distill

Quiet your thoughts. Turn your ear toward Him. What is the primary thing He has said to you? Trust what you hear Him say to you. Write it down.

  _____

  _____

  _____

~ Day 19 ~

Delight Yourself in Him

"How great is the love the Father has lavished on us, that we should be called children of God!" (1 John 3:1). Think of it. He has made you His child. Consider all that entails. Let the thought usher your soul into sabbath.

Discover

Abraham in hope believed. . . . Being fully persuaded
that God had power to do what he had promised.
(Rom. 4:18–21)

Abraham, our faith-father, is offered as the supreme example of how confidence in God's power and provision operates. In Abraham's mind, God's word carried more weight than the appearance of his circumstances.

> Against all hope, Abraham in hope believed and so became the father of many nations, just as it had been said to him, "So shall your offspring be." Without weakening in his faith, he faced the fact that his body was as good as dead—since he was about a hundred years old—and that Sarah's womb was also dead. Yet he did not waver through unbelief regarding the promise of God, but was strengthened in his faith and gave glory to God, being fully persuaded that God had power to do what he had promised. (Rom. 4:18–21)

As surely as God promised Abraham a son and heir, God has promised you that He will meet your needs. You can rest assured that any need in your life has been allowed by God. He has given permission for that need to come into your experience. He is going to use it as a platform for His power. Here is the key to resting in the midst of what seems to be unmet needs: *God has the power to do what He has promised.*

Let's look at Abraham's example. At a certain point in his experience, it appeared that God's promise and the reality of Abraham's situation were mutually exclusive. God had promised an heir. Both Abraham's and Sarah's childbearing potential had past. "He faced the fact that his body was as good as dead . . . and that Sarah's womb was also dead" (Rom. 4:19). But Abraham knew the Promiser. He knew that Jehovah had the power to bring life out of death.

Paul wrote that at the moment in Abraham's faith journey that the vision seemed most impossible, he "was strengthened in his faith." The passive tense of the verb here indicates the subject, Abraham, was acted upon. Abraham did not strengthen his own faith; he allowed his faith to be strengthened. He opened his life to God's presence, which strengthened him.

God Himself will strengthen you. He will enlarge your faith. Even while your circumstances seem to stay the same; even when it seems that the opportunity for God to act has passed; even then, God will strengthen your faith. He will enable you to believe Him. He will empower you to trust Him. He will repeat His promises to your heart over and over again until they take root. Don't struggle. Don't work at it. Rest. Sabbath.

As you keep your life open to the flow of His power, He will supply your every need. Ask Him, and He will gladly give you everything you need and fulfill your heart's true desire. He is looking for opportunities to prove His word to you.

• What needs are in your life? Why has God allowed them?

_____

_____

_____

_____

• Is He able to meet your needs?

_____

_____

_____

• Is He willing to meet your needs?

_____

_____

_____

• What, if anything, might be blocking the flow of His power and provision in your life? What do you need to do about it?

_____

_____

_____

Distill

Quiet your thoughts. Turn your ear toward Him. What is the primary thing He has said to you? Trust what you hear Him say to you. Write it down.

_____

_____

_____

~ Day 20 ~

Review and Reflect

- Why did God create you with needs?

  _____

  _____

  _____

- Why, if God knows what we need before we ask Him, does He instruct us to ask for them?

  _____

  _____

  _____

- Is there anything more that God needs to do to prove that He loves you and wants to provide all your needs?

  _____

  _____

  _____

- What have you learned of Him this week that helps you move into soul-sabbath?

  _____

  _____

  _____

• What does this verse mean to you?

He who did not spare his own Son, but gave him up for us all—how will he not also, along with him, graciously give us all things? (Rom. 8:32)

_____

_____

_____

~ *Day 21* ~

Journal Your Thoughts and Prayers

_____

_____

_____

_____

_____

_____

_____

_____

_____

_____

_____

_____

_____

_____

_____

_____

_____

_____

_____

WEEK 4

Forgive

"'Forgive us our debts,
as we also have forgiven our debtors.'"
(Matt. 6:12)

When Jesus took on the weight of your sin and carried it to the cross, He also carried the sins committed against you. When you insist on holding on to
the hurts inflicted on you, you deny the power of
His crucifixion.

~ *Day 22* ~

Delight Yourself in Him

"They will be called oaks of righteousness, / a planting of the LORD / for the display of his splendor" (Isa. 61:3). The peace He is planting in you will cause your soul to be as steady and as deeply rooted as a mighty oak tree. The stillness of your heart puts His splendor on display. Delight in His strength that flows through you.

Discover

"'Forgive us our debts,
as we also have forgiven our debtors.'"
(Matt. 6:12)

Jesus, in His prayer outline, tied together the forgiveness we receive from the Father and the forgiveness we offer to others. One is the outgrowth of the other. Because we have received forgiveness, we extend forgiveness.

The Greek word translated "forgive" means "to send off" or "to send away." The act of forgiving separates the sin from the one who sinned. It "sends away" the sin, with its penalty and its attendant guilt. This transaction was pictured in the Old Testament by the sacrificial system. The guilty person made a sin offering or guilt offering with an unblemished animal from his own livestock. Before killing the animal, he laid his hands on the animal. He leaned into the animal with all his weight. This symbolized laying his sins on the animal; the animal was bearing the "weight" of his sins. Then he killed the animal, recognizing that the wages of sin is death. As that person leaned his weight upon the sacrificial animal, Yaweh declared, "'"It will be accepted on his behalf to make atonement for him"'" (Lev. 1:4). The sin was separated from the one who sinned because it was placed on the sacrifice.

The forgiveness we receive from the Father is not a passive act but instead is a costly transaction. Your forgiveness and my forgiveness from the Father is available because "the LORD has laid on him / the iniquity of us all" (Isa. 53:6). Do you see? God separated you from your sin. He took the sin off of you and placed it on the Son. He sent your sin away. The One who knew no sin became sin for us. It is finished and settled. Lean the weight of your sin on Him who took your sin to the cross. You are forgiven.

> It was for me
> He took on the time and space constraints of earth
> Let a veil of flesh conceal His worth
> Set redemption's plan in motion with His birth.
> It was for me.
>
> It was for me
> He gave up His flesh—an offering for my sin
> Let God's wrath toward me be spent on Him
> Poured out His life so my life could begin.
> It was for me.
>
> It was for me
> He threw off the time and space constraints of earth
> Shed His veil of flesh, revealed His worth
> Opened up for me the way to Spirit birth.
> It was for me.[10]

How much He loves you! The act of sacrifice—the sacrifice of the Son and the sacrifice of the Father—was not a generic, impersonal action, but a specific, directed, intimate action *on your behalf.* The Father's love for you is as personal as if you were His only love.

Have you received His love fully in accepting His forgiveness? Or do you continue to hold on to guilt and shame? Do you hang your head in His presence? Or have you discovered Him as "the One who lifts my head" (Ps. 3:3, NASB)?

- Are you struggling with guilt for past sins? Right now, lean the weight of that sin on Him. See in your heart that He took it upon Himself to the cross. Look at the scene until the truth of it settles in.

- Name the past sins that He bore the weight of for you. Write them down. Let them go.

_____

_____

_____

Distill

Quiet your thoughts. Turn your ear toward Him. What is the primary thing He has said to you? Trust what you hear Him say to you. Write it down.

_____

_____

_____

~ Day 23 ~

Delight Yourself in Him

"The fruit of righteousness will be peace; / the effect of righteousness will be quietness and confidence forever" (Isa. 32:17). Jesus Himself is your righteousness. The effect of His life in you is peace, quietness, and confidence. Be still and let a solid awareness of confidence fill your heart.

Discover

He forgave us all our sins, having canceled the written code,
with its regulations, that was against us and that stood opposed to us;
he took it away, nailing it to the cross.
(Col. 2:13–14)

This Scripture describes our condition before we entered into relationship with Christ as being dead in our trespasses and sins (Eph. 2:1; 2:5; Col. 2:13). Why? Because we had a death sentence pronounced against us by the law. The law was based on the fact that sin brings death. Therefore, being under a sentence of death, we were like a "dead man walking."[11] In Christ, the Father resurrected us. He reversed the death sentence, pardoned us, and even canceled the "written code"—the law that pronounced our death sentence. The law accused us and condemned us to death—it "stood opposed to us." But Jesus Christ nailed it to the cross.

When Jesus hung on the cross—when He poured out His life on my behalf—He carried out my death sentence. "You also died to the law through the body of Christ" (Rom. 7:4). He did not nullify the law; He fulfilled the law. The law was just and right in pronouncing a death sentence against me. My death sentence *was carried out.* On Him. When He fulfilled the demands of the law on my behalf, I then became free from the law's authority to pronounce punishment against me. When He died my death for me, the "me" who was under a death sentence no longer existed. That "me" died. A new "me" was born. "But now, by dying to what once bound us, we have been released from the law so that we serve in the new way of the Spirit, and not in the old way of the written code" (Rom. 7:6). The written code is cancelled. I am alive and free to live by the power of the indwelling, resurrected Christ.

I am forgiven. You are forgiven. He took your sin off of you—separated your sin from you—and nailed it to the cross. It is paid for. You are free.

Does the enemy—the accuser—try to steal your peace by reminding you of your sins? Does he bring disquiet into your thoughts and restlessness into your emotions? Does he condemn you and discourage you and convince you that the Father cannot possibly lavish His love on someone like you? Reject his lies and distortions. Believe and count on the truth. "Who will bring any charge against those whom God has chosen? It is God who justifies" (Rom. 8:33). Bring your thoughts into alignment with the true facts. Enter into the sabbath-rest—the finished work. You are forgiven.

- What does it mean to you to be forgiven?

  _____

  _____

- Make this your prayer: *Father, I know that You love me, accept me, delight in me, and treasure me. I know that I am clean in Your sight. I know that You are not holding anything against me. I know that Your love for me is steady and certain.*

Distill

Quiet your thoughts. Turn your ear toward Him. What is the primary thing He has said to you? Trust what you hear Him say to you. Write it down.

_____

_____

~ Day 24 ~

Delight Yourself in Him

"'Let the beloved of the LORD rest secure in him, / for he shields him all day long, / and the one the LORD loves rests between his shoulders'" (Deut. 33:12). You are the beloved of the Lord. You are the one the Lord loves. Rest in Him.

Discover

"And when you stand praying, if you hold anything
against anyone, forgive him, so that your Father in heaven
may forgive you your sins."
(Mark 11:25)

Choosing not to forgive others is closing the door to God's forgiveness. This does *not* mean that when you do not forgive, God withholds His forgiveness as a punishment. It does *not* mean that you earn your forgiveness by forgiving others. If this were so, it would directly contradict the entire gospel message. Your forgiveness is a settled matter, settled at the cross. You've already seen that Christ's death in your place fulfilled your obligation and erased your debt. God will not go back on His Word. Yet, this concept tying your forgiveness of those who wrong you to God's forgiveness of you is repeated and emphasized by Jesus. So we must come to an understanding of what it means.

Foundational to this understanding is the recognition of how much God has forgiven you. If you were the only person ever to commit a sin, Jesus would still have died for you. It still would have taken His death on the cross to pay for your sins alone. When He died on the cross, it was for your sins. The Father has forgiven you more than you will ever be called upon to forgive any other person. The cost of His forgiveness is a higher price than you will ever have to pay. No matter what anyone has ever done to you, that person's sin against you does not come close to the measure of your sins against God.

Second, it is not you who does the forgiving. The Father living in you does His work (see John 14:10). You, on your own, have neither the inclination nor the ability to forgive. You are the conduit of His forgiveness. Holding on to anger cuts off the flow of His power through you. It clogs the channel through which His love flows.

Third, understand that when Jesus said "so that your Father in heaven may forgive you your sins," He did not refer to the action of forgiving—which Jesus knew would be finished at the cross—but instead referred to having His forgiveness in your experience. He wants forgiveness to move from being an abstract theological concept to being your truth. Deliberately nursing a grievance, holding it close and giving it nourishment, keeps the reality of the Father's forgiveness from you. When you choose to hold on to anger or bitterness, you refuse to let go of a sin—the sin of unforgiveness. It is the confessing and turning from a sin that brings the Father's forgiveness into your experience.

The Scripture tells us that deliberate unforgiveness gives the enemy an opening. Paul wrote: "What I have forgiven—if there was anything to forgive—I have forgiven in the sight of Christ for your sake, *in order that Satan might not outwit us.* For we are not unaware of his schemes" (2 Cor. 2:10–11, italics added). As you forgive those who have wronged you, you close the door to Satan's schemes and you open the door to the power of God.

You can have the peace that comes from forgiving others and letting go of the turmoil that anger and resentment bring to your emotions. When you believe what God says about the high price of your forgiveness, you will be ready to forgive anybody anything. Forgive and let the peace of Christ stand guard over your heart.

- What or whom are you struggling to forgive?

  _____

  _____

  _____

- Do you want to be free of the bitterness and the anger? If you do, ask the Father to do His work in you and through you? Write it out.

  _____

  _____

  _____

- Be patient with the process as the Father heals. You are in His hands. Don't take the burden on yourself.

Distill

Quiet your thoughts. Turn your ear toward Him. What is the primary thing He has said to you? Trust what you hear Him say to you. Write it down.

  _____

  _____

  _____

~ Day 25 ~

Delight Yourself in Him

"'I am sending you grain, new wine and oil, / enough to satisfy you fully'" (Joel 2:19). In the symbolic language of Scripture, bread or grain most often represents Jesus, the Bread of Life, and both oil and wine usually picture the Holy Spirit. The Father is providing you all your soul needs to be fully satisfied. Take what He is offering.

Discover

Be kind and compassionate to one another, forgiving each other,
just as in Christ God forgave you.
(Eph. 4:32)

The model for how you and I are to forgive is God Himself. Remember that it is His forgiveness being poured out through you. Examine the Father's forgiveness that He displayed through Jesus.

1. He forgives completely.

    "For I will forgive their wickedness
      and will remember their sins no more." (Heb. 8:12)
    And where these have been forgiven, there is no longer any
      sacrifice for sin. (Heb. 10:18)

2. He forgave us when we didn't deserve it and didn't even desire it.

    But God demonstrates his own love for us in this: While we
    were still sinners, Christ died for us. (Rom. 5:8)

3. He forgives time and time again.

   "If he sins against you seven times in a day, and seven times comes back to you and says, 'I repent,' forgive him." (Luke 17:4)

4. He begins the forgiving process even while the offense is in progress.

   When they came to the place called the Skull, there they crucified him, along with the criminals—one on his right, the other on his left. Jesus said, "Father, forgive them, for they do not know what they are doing." (Luke 23:33–34)

I have found Jesus' words, "they do not know what they are doing," to be extremely important in learning to forgive. I believe this is nearly always true. The one who offended you does not really know what he or she is doing. A large percentage of the offenses against us are entirely unintentional. Most of the time, your offender has no idea how you have perceived his actions or words. You, in fact, have hurt or offended others unintentionally. How many of the hurts that you are struggling with are really your perceptions of a situation or a comment? How much of the anger you have against others is really the result of feelings, attitudes, or intentions that you are projecting on other people? Forgive them. They do not know what they are doing.

Even when a person's words or actions are deliberately unkind or harsh, as were the soldiers' who were crucifying Jesus, the person does not fully understand the ramifications. Strange as it seems, even a person who appears to be intentionally harming you has been blinded by the enemy to the whole picture. Your enemy is not flesh and blood. The human heart is deceitful—able to fool itself. Forgive him. Forgive her. Let it go. They do not know what they are doing.

- Look at the hurts you are having trouble letting go of. Is it possible that your offender is unaware of how he or she has hurt you?

  _____

  _____

  _____

- Even if you feel the offense was intentional and even meant to cause you pain, can you understand that your offender may be blind to truth and, in his or her own mind, does not see the offense for what it is? Will you accept that? Write out what you are feeling and thinking.

  _____

  _____

  _____

- When you can, choose to pray: *Father, forgive* _____. *He/she does not know what he/she is doing.*

Distill

Quiet your thoughts. Turn your ear toward Him. What is the primary thing He has said to you? Trust what you hear Him say to you. Write it down.

  _____

  _____

  _____

~ Day 26 ~

Delight Yourself in Him

"The LORD bless you and keep you; the LORD make his face shine upon you and be gracious to you; the LORD turn his face toward you and give you peace" (Num. 6:24–26). With the eyes of your heart, look into His face. Peace is there.

Discover

Surely our griefs He Himself bore,
And our sorrows He carried.
(Isa. 53:4, NASB)

You were not designed to carry anger and bitterness. It weighs you down and holds you back. Because the Father loves you, He does not want you bearing a burden that is not yours to bear.

When Jesus took on the weight of your sin and carried it to the cross, He also carried the sins committed against you. When you insist on holding on to the hurts inflicted on you, you deny the power of His crucifixion. He died for *sinners,* for the *ungodly.* "You see, at just the right time, when we were still powerless, Christ died for the ungodly. . . . God demonstrates his own love for us in this: While we were still sinners, Christ died for us" (Rom. 5:6–8). Is your offender a sinner? Christ died for his sins. Is your offender ungodly? Christ died for her. Extend grace—the same grace that God extended to you.

Not only did He carry your sin, but He bore the weight of your grief and your sorrows. He bore the hurt of the sins committed against you. Just as you have leaned the weight of your sins on Him, now lean the weight of your grief and your sorrow on Him. Let Him pick it up and carry it. It is too heavy for you.

By bearing the weight of your own hurt, you allow the offense to continue and to multiply its effect on you. You may be passing the hurt along to others in your life. The offense grows and spreads. "See to it that no one misses the grace of God and that no bitter root grows up to cause trouble and defile many" (Heb. 12:15). If bitterness is allowed to take root in you, it will begin to grow fruit. Your actions, words, attitudes, responses will be bitter fruit growing from a bitter root. It will create bitterness in those who are exposed to it. One offense can poison many people, even spreading from generation to generation. Do you really want to enable your offender to have access to so many lives? Wouldn't it be better to forgive and let your life produce the fruit of the Spirit instead?

What is the cure for bitterness?

> When they came to Marah, they could not drink its water because it was bitter. (That is why the place is called Marah.) So the people grumbled against Moses, saying, "What are we to drink?"
>
> Then Moses cried out to the LORD, and the LORD showed him a piece of wood. He threw it into the water, and the water became sweet. (Exod. 15:23–25)

The cross is the cure for bitterness. Let your bitterness come into contact with the cross of Jesus. Just as Moses threw the wood into the midst of the bitter waters, let the cross of Christ take center stage in your circumstances. Let the effect of His crucifixion and the power of His resurrection heal any bitterness in you. Let that which flows from you be sweet rivers of Living Water. Let those who come in contact with you be exposed to life instead of death. Let them sense peace instead of turmoil; rest instead of restlessness. Let your soul live in sabbath.

- Lean the weight of your grief and hurt on Him. Let Him have it. He has taken it to the cross. Let go of it. Sit still and let the reality of the cross take hold of you. Feel the hurt and grief let go of your heart.

Write out your thoughts.

_____

_____

_____

_____

_____

Distill

Quiet your thoughts. Turn your ear toward Him. What is the primary thing He has said to you? Trust what you hear Him say to you. Write it down.

_____

_____

_____

~ Day 27 ~

Review and Reflect

- What is the literal meaning of the word *forgive?*

  _____

  _____

  _____

- What has the word *forgive* meant to you as you have spent time sabbathing in the Lord's presence this week?

  _____

  _____

  _____

- What specific issue came to mind again and again this week?

  _____

  _____

  _____

- What resolution have you reached about it?

  _____

  _____

  _____

- What does this verse mean to you?

Be kind and compassionate to one another, forgiving each other, just as in Christ God forgave you. (Eph. 4:32)

_____

_____

_____

~ Day 28 ~

Journal Your Thoughts and Prayers

_____

_____

_____

_____

_____

_____

_____

_____

_____

_____

_____

_____

_____

_____

_____

_____

_____

_____

_____

WEEK 5

Lead Us Not into Temptation

"'And lead us not into temptation,
but deliver us from the evil one.'"
(Matt. 6:13)

When you pray, "Lead me not into temptation," you
can be assured that any testing circumstances that
come your way are for the purpose of enriching you
and causing you to put down deeper roots in the soil
of faith. He will not allow you to be subjected to
unnecessary testing.

~ Day 29 ~

Delight Yourself in Him

"I will make peace your governor / and righteousness your ruler" (Isa. 60:17). The Scripture speaks often of peace and righteousness as companions. Righteousness is inner peace; it is being in harmony with truth. Unrighteousness is kicking against the goads (see Acts 26:14). Let Him give peace to govern your life and righteousness to rule you.

Discover

"'And lead us not into temptation,
but deliver us from the evil one.'"
(Matt. 6:13)

"'Why are you sleeping?' [Jesus] asked them. 'Get up and pray so that you will not fall into temptation'" (Luke 22:46). The Greek word translated "temptation" also means "testing, trial, proving." During those emotionally charged hours before His arrest, Jesus urgently reminded His disciples to strengthen themselves through prayer against the onslaught of testing headed their way. That openness to the flow of God's power and provision (prayer) would provide the victory in the moment of testing. When the moment came for proving what was on the inside, the battle the disciples faced could have been won in the prayer that preceded it.

At least twice during His prayer vigil Jesus admonished His disciples with these words. Don't you think that this gives us some insight into the spiritual battle in which Jesus was engaged during His Gethsemane hours? The moment was approaching for which His whole purpose in coming to earth would be put to the test. His mission would be tested and proven. Jesus, during His period of agonized praying, received from the Father the strength, assurance, endurance, courage, and confidence to face the temptation—more accurately, the trial—and not fall. His mental, emotional, and spiritual serenity throughout His crucifixion experience was birthed in the hours of prayer and the life of prayer that preceded it.

> True praying involves serious attention and time, which flesh and blood do not relish. Few people have such strong fiber that they will make a costly outlay when inferior work will pass just as well in the marketplace.
>
> To be little with God is to be little for God. It takes much time for the fullness of God to flow into the spirit. Short devotions cut the pipe of God's flow. We live shabbily because we pray meagerly.[12]
>
> E. M. Bounds, *The Necessity of Prayer*

Did the Father lead Him into that trial? The record of Scripture is clear. Evil persons with evil intent made and carried out their evil plans. Satan, in fact, orchestrated the events. Yet all of the decisions and actions lined up with the timetable and the purposes God had laid out and announced throughout history (see Acts 2:23). Jesus, doing only what the Father showed Him to do, found Himself in the midst of the ultimate testing. His praying life, however, prepared Him and focused Him so that at the moment of testing He did not fall.

He had already taught His disciples to pray, "Lead us not into temptation." Let me paraphrase for you what I think that petition means: *When my path leads me through times of proving—authenticating what is inside me—hold me so that I do not fall. When Satan asks and receives permission to sift me like wheat, keep me from falling into his trap.* Living in this attitude of dependence upon Him readies you for the circumstances that take you by surprise, giving Him the opportunity to prove His sufficiency.

- Are you satisfied with the amount of time you are giving to focused prayer? If not, what keeps you from it?

  _____

  _____

  _____

- Do you truly believe that prayer is the most important activity you can engage in? Explain your answer.

  _____

  _____

  _____

- Why must a praying life be nourished and undergirded by daily times of focused, intentional prayer?

  _____

  _____

  _____

Distill

Quiet your thoughts. Turn your ear toward Him. What is the primary thing He has said to you? Trust what you hear Him say to you. Write it down.

_____

_____

_____

~ Day 30 ~

Delight Yourself in Him

"He who dwells in the shelter of the Most High / will rest in the shadow of the Almighty" (Ps. 91:1). Let your soul rest in His presence. Feel the calm flow of the still waters in you and around you.

Discover

God is faithful; he will not let you be tempted
beyond what you can bear.
(1 Cor. 10:13)

Look carefully at what the Scripture says about temptation: God will not *let you* be tempted beyond what you can bear. Do you see that God is in charge of what temptation reaches you? If God is in charge of what temptation reaches you, can temptation have any purpose but good? "All the ways of the LORD are loving and faithful / for those who keep the demands of his covenant" (Ps. 25:10). "You are good, and what you do is good" (Ps. 119:68).

Everything in your life serves God's purpose. "Your laws endure to this day, / for *all things serve you*" (Ps. 119:91, italics added). Everything—including temptation—serves God's purpose. What is God's purpose? What eternal good is He accomplishing through allowing temptation?

First, let me backtrack and clarify something. God does not tempt you. He is not the source of temptation. "When tempted, no one should say, 'God is tempting me.' For God cannot be tempted by evil, nor does he tempt anyone" (James 1:13). He does, however, decide what temptation will be allowed to reach you.

What is God's purpose in allowing temptation? What is His goal?

"If we confess our sins, he is faithful and just and will forgive us our sins and purify us from all unrighteousness" (1 John 1:9). God wants to do more than forgive our sins! God wants to: (1) forgive our sins, and (2) purify us from all unrighteousness. The Word of God, then, specifies two dimensions of impurity. He will deal with *sins* by forgiving them and with *unrighteousness* by purifying it. He will deal with the fruit (sins) and the root that produces the fruit. Sins are the behaviors we engage in. Unrighteousness is the attitude of rebellion that causes us to sin. When God deals with the root, the fruit ceases to exist. God allows temptation in order to isolate, identify, and uproot unrighteousness.

Temptation is not sin. Temptation can lead to sin, or temptation can lead to purity. Temptation forces choice. Temptation shows us the places at which we are still responsive to sin. Temptation is a heart EKG. It pinpoints the weak places. Temptation exposes impurities. It unmasks our hearts so that sin cannot lurk there undetected. Temptation forces sin into the light where it can be destroyed.

When Jesus taught us to pray, "Lead us not into temptation," He was not teaching us that God will keep us from exposure to temptation. Rather, temptation that God allows will work to our benefit and will work out His purposes. When we are confronted with temptation in the course of a praying life, we can rise above it rather than falling into it.

• Where has temptation revealed the weak places in your heart to be?

_____

_____

_____

- When confronted with temptation, do you immediately consider yourself weak? What would happen if you let temptation reveal your strength instead?

  _____

  _____

  _____

- Redefine *temptation.* It is not so much an enticement to sin as it is an opportunity to loosen sin's hold and uproot unrighteousness. Write out a spiritual strategy that you will employ when next you are confronted with a familiar temptation.

  _____

  _____

  _____

  _____

  _____

Distill

Quiet your thoughts. Turn your ear toward Him. What is the primary thing He has said to you? Trust what you hear Him say to you. Write it down.

_____

_____

_____

~ Day 31 ~

Delight Yourself in Him

"The plans of the Lord stand firm forever, the purposes of his heart through all generations" (Ps. 33:11). You can rest in the Lord because He is changelessly good. His plans and the purposes of His heart can be relied on. Let His steadfastness impart peace to your heart and rest to your soul.

Discover

For our light and momentary troubles
are achieving for us an eternal glory
that far outweighs them all.
(2 Cor. 4:17)

The proving and authenticating the Father does in our lives sometimes comes through His allowing us to be directly tempted to engage in sin. Other times it comes through the testing of circumstances. How can belief mature into faith except by putting it to the test?

God wants you to have "full assurance of faith" (Heb. 10:22). What is faith? "Now faith is being *sure* of what we hope for and *certain* of what we do not see" (Heb. 11:1, italics added). Belief is something else. Belief is the starting point for faith, but belief is not faith. Faith is born of first-hand experience.

You can only know Him by firsthand experience. Knowing God produces faith. You cannot trust the promises. You must trust the Promiser. A promise is only as reliable as the person who makes it. If you don't know the promiser, you have no way of knowing whether or not to rely on the promise. "Let us hold unswervingly to the hope we profess, for *he who promised* is faithful" (Heb. 10:23). In order to live by faith, we have to be "fully persuaded that God [has] power to do what he [has] promised" (Rom. 4:21).

Faith can only come through a direct, firsthand encounter with Jesus. Belief can come through secondhand information, but belief is not faith. I can believe things without putting my faith in them. For example, I can believe that a chair will hold me up. However, if I never sit in the chair—if I never put my faith in it—I will never move from belief to certain knowledge. Why does that matter?

Let's say that I believe that a certain chair will hold me up, but I have never sat in that chair. I am in the "belief" position. Now my adversary can say, "That chair will never hold you up."

"Of course it will. I believe it will," I reply.

"How do you know?" my adversary taunts.

"Because I can see that it is constructed of sturdy materials. I can see where the center of gravity would be. I'm sure the chair would hold me up."

Then my adversary could say, "But there may be a hidden flaw you don't know about."

My only answer could be, "You're right. There could be."

Belief can be shaken. Faith cannot.

Suppose that I take the faith position and sit in the chair. Now my adversary can say, "That chair will never hold you up." To which I will reply, "Of course it will."

My adversary will then say, "How do you know?" And I will reply, "Because it is."

I will overcome his attack with the word of my testimony. Faith cannot be shaken. Faith comes from firsthand experience.

Suppose that I came to earth from another planet with the assignment of learning all I can about the earth. Suppose that I wanted to learn about earth rocks. Someone tells me, "Earth rocks are hard." That becomes what I believe. With all my heart, I believe that earth rocks are hard. However, no matter how much emotion I invest in my belief, it is only belief. It came to me secondhand, and secondhand information can only produce belief.

Suppose that someone else told me later that earth rocks are soft and spongy. Now what would I believe? I'd sometimes lean toward believing that rocks were hard, and other times I'd be convinced that they were soft. I'd be like a wave of the sea, blown and tossed by the wind. I'd waver between two opinions.

What would be the one and only remedy for my dilemma? I would have to touch an earth rock for myself. Then I would know—not just believe—that earth rocks are hard. Never again would I wonder if they're really soft. I would have faith that earth rocks are hard. Faith cannot be shaken.[13]

When God allows difficult circumstances into your life, know that He has determined that the glory they will produce outweighs the pain they will cause. You will have the opportunity to move from belief to faith. When you pray, "Lead me not into temptation," you can be assured that any testing circumstances that come your way are for the purpose of enriching you and causing you to put down deeper roots in the soil of faith. He will not subject you to unnecessary testing.

This prayer, then, does not surface from a desire to hide from any difficulty or challenge. The person who prays this prayer in the context of a praying life asks that any oncoming test will be one that will move him closer to his goal—the goal he shares with the Father—to be conformed to the image of the Son. Until this is the focus and the intent of his life, the testings that come his way will fail to yield that "weight of glory" they were meant to produce.

My goal is God Himself, not joy, nor peace,
   Nor even blessing, but Himself, my God;
'Tis His to lead me there, not mine, but His—
   "At any cost, dear Lord, by any road."[14]

- What opportunities do you have in your life right now to put faith to the test?

_____

_____

_____

- How can you cooperate with God's purpose for you as you respond to these opportunities?

_____

_____

_____

Distill

Quiet your thoughts. Turn your ear toward Him. What is the primary thing He has said to you? Trust what you hear Him say to you. Write it down.

_____

_____

_____

~ *Day 32* ~

Delight Yourself in the Lord

"Let the light of your face shine upon us, O Lord. / You have filled my heart with greater joy / than when their grain and new wine abound" (Ps. 4:6–7). As you learn more how to live in sabbath, you discover your heart is filled with a supernatural joy, rest, and peace that has nothing to do with circumstances. Sit quietly and let that inner peace fill you as the light of His face shines on you.

Discover

"'Deliver us from the evil one.'"
(Matt. 6:13)

The outcome of having not fallen into temptation is that we are delivered from the evil one. The word *deliver (rhuomai)* means "to draw or snatch from danger, rescue, deliver. This is more with the meaning of drawing to oneself than merely rescuing from someone or something."[15]

Your enemy engineers and instigates temptations and difficulties to defeat you. Keep in mind that he conceives of and tries to inflict on you many, many more difficulties than those God allows. God keeps you from nearly all of Satan's plans against you, allowing only those that will accomplish His own purpose in you. Those that God does allow, He does not allow in full measure. He screens them, filtering out the elements that will not work toward His ends. When you find yourself in difficult, even devastating circumstances, God will deliver you from your enemy's plan for defeat and, in the midst of it, will draw you to Himself.

Your triumph over Satan and his forces has already been accomplished. Following God, you are assured the victory before the battle begins. Before the opening shots are fired, the outcome is certain. The Scripture proclaims He "always leads us in triumphal procession in Christ" (2 Cor. 2:14).

The sixth chapter of Joshua portrays an interesting story. To possess the Promised Land, the Israelites needed to take the city of Jericho. Jericho was protected by a high and impenetrable wall. "Now Jericho was tightly shut up because of the Israelites. No one went out and no one came in" (Josh. 6:1). Imagine the Israelites as they looked at the walls of Jericho. Imagine how they must have evaluated the empirical evidence confronting them. "Impossible! We're defeated before we start," they might have decided.

God had a different viewpoint. "Then the LORD said to Joshua, 'See, I have delivered Jericho into your hands'" (Josh. 6:2). In the material realm, this was not the case. In the material realm, the Israelites were positioned outside the walls of Jericho looking at a fortress that was overwhelming and beyond their abilities to conquer. Notice that God did not say, "I *will deliver* Jericho." He said, "I *have delivered* Jericho into your hands." God spoke of a completed reality. Then God gave Joshua the directives that would bring that victory into their experience, recorded in verses 3–5. "By faith the walls of Jericho fell, after the people had marched around them for seven days" (Heb. 11:30).

God has not allowed a battle into your life that has not already been fought and won at the cross. When you lean on Him, rest in Him and His finished work—His sabbath—He will deliver you from the evil one. It is certain.

- Look at the difficult circumstances that confront you today. While you are looking at them with your mind's eye, hear the Father say, "I have delivered this battle into your hands. The triumphal procession has already begun. Get in step with it." Write out your thoughts and responses.

_____

_____

_____

Distill

Quiet your thoughts. Turn your ear toward Him. What is the primary thing He has said to you? Trust what you hear Him say to you. Write it down.

_____

_____

_____

~ Day 33 ~

Delight Yourself in the Lord

"'In your unfailing love you will lead / the people you have redeemed. / In your strength you will guide them / to your holy dwelling'" (Exod. 15:13). Rest in this: God is bringing you to the goal. Don't put your faith in your commitment, or your faith, or your willingness. Put your faith in His unfailing love and His strength. He will finish what He has started.

Discover

Put on the full armor of God so that you
can take your stand against the devil's schemes.
(Eph. 6:11)

God has provided for your deliverance. All of His work is finished. It is ready. His deliverance is Jesus.

The word translated "put on" in Ephesians 6:11 means "to envelop in; to hide in." Put on the full armor of God. Be enveloped in it. Hide in it. "All of you who were baptized into Christ have clothed yourselves with Christ" (Gal. 3:27).

Note that every single piece of the armor Paul listed in Ephesians 6 is Jesus:

Truth

"I am the way and the truth and the life." (John 14:6)

Righteousness

It is because of him that you are in Christ Jesus, who has become for us wisdom from God—that is, our righteousness, holiness and redemption. (1 Cor. 1:30)

Gospel of Peace

    For he himself is our peace. (Eph. 2:14)

    We have peace with God through our Lord Jesus Christ. (Rom. 5:1)

Faith

    Let us fix our eyes on Jesus, the author and perfecter of our faith. (Heb. 12:2)

Salvation

    In bringing many sons to glory, it was fitting that God, for whom and through whom everything exists, should make the author of their salvation perfect through suffering. (Heb. 2:10)

    He became the source of eternal salvation for all who obey him. (Heb. 5:9)

Word of God

    In the beginning was the Word, and the Word was with God, and the Word was God. He was with God in the beginning. (John 1:1–2)

Another way of saying to put on the whole armor of God is "clothe yourselves with the Lord Jesus Christ" (Rom. 13:14).

Jesus said from the cross, "It is finished." He used a word that means "to bring to a close; to complete; to carry out a command." He completed His mission. He accomplished what He was supposed to accomplish. He became everything we ever needed and would ever need. He is the finished work of the Father. He is the Sabbath. He is the Rest. He is the eternal I Am.

Put on the whole Armor of God.

- Read through Ephesians 6:13–18 below. At each piece of the armor, stop and recognize it as Jesus. Underline it and write "Jesus" over it.

Confess Him as the finished work—all you need. Mentally, put on each piece of armor.

Therefore put on the full armor of God, so that when the day of evil comes, you may be able to stand your ground, and after you have done everything, to stand. Stand firm then, with the belt of truth buckled around your waist, with the breastplate of righteousness in place, and with your feet fitted with the readiness that comes from the gospel of peace. In addition to all this, take up the shield of faith, with which you can extinguish all the flaming arrows of the evil one. Take the helmet of salvation and the sword of the Spirit, which is the word of God. And pray in the Spirit on all occasions with all kinds of prayers and requests.

Distill

Quiet your thoughts. Turn your ear toward Him. What is the primary thing He has said to you? Trust what you hear Him say to you. Write it down.

_____

_____

_____

~ Day 34 ~

Review and Reflect

- What does it mean to you when you pray, "Lead me not into temptation"?

_____

_____

_____

- How does this prayer fit into the landscape of a praying life?

_____

_____

_____

- When you have full assurance that the Father can and will keep you from unnecessary testing, how will you face the situations that come into your life to authenticate your faith?

_____

_____

_____

- What is the difference between belief and faith? How does belief become faith?

_____

_____

_____

- What does this verse mean to you?

  For our light and momentary troubles are achieving for us an eternal glory that far outweighs them all. (2 Cor. 4:17)

  _____

  _____

  _____

~ Day 35 ~

Journal Your Thoughts and Prayers

_____

_____

_____

_____

_____

_____

_____

_____

_____

_____

_____

_____

_____

_____

_____

_____

_____

_____

_____

_____

WEEK 6

The Kingdom, the Power, and the Glory

"'For yours is the kingdom and the power and the glory forever.'"
(Matt. 6:13)

The kingdom has only one secret, but this secret will change everything. It will usher you into unending soul-sabbath.

~ Day 36 ~

Delight Yourself in Him

"I run in the path of your commands, / for you have set my heart free" (Ps. 119:32). As He frees you from anxiety, from bitterness, from uncertainty, from everything that would hold you captive, you will run in the path of His commands. More and more you will realize that this is the way of freedom. This is the way of peace. Celebrate your heart's freedom.

Discover

"For yours is the kingdom and the power and the glory forever."
(Matt. 6:13) [16]

Praise is the foundation of prayer. All prayer is to be wrapped in praise and thanksgiving.

> Do not be anxious about anything, but in everything, by prayer and petition, with thanksgiving, present your requests to God. And the peace of God, which transcends all understanding, will guard your hearts and your minds in Christ Jesus. (Phil. 4:6–7)

Do not be anxious about *anything*. Are there any limits to this injunction to be anxiety-free?

The Israelites found themselves between the advancing Egyptian army and the Red Sea (see Exod. 14). They looked around, took stock of the situation and reached the only logical conclusion: "We're going to die!" But they were about to embark on a forty-year lesson.

Don't define the situation by what you can see. Don't evaluate your options based on the earth-viewpoint. Don't think that your circumstances are the whole picture.

God addressed the people through His spokesman, Moses. The first thing He said was, "Do not fear." He knew that their circumstances looked fearful. He understood that from their perspective, fear was the only logical emotion. For this reason His opening words to them were, "Do not fear."

What are the circumstances in your life right now that cause you to be anxious and fearful? What is it that looks hopeless to you?

Listen to the Father: *"Do not fear. There's more to this than meets the eye. If you could see it through My eyes, you would not be afraid. You can rest in My finished work. You can sabbath."*

Then He continued, "Stand firm and you will see the deliverance the LORD will bring you today." How had the Israelites come to this place? The Lord had led them there: they were exactly where God wanted them to be. God had engineered the whole situation.

Read Exodus 14:1–4:

Then the Lord said to Moses, "Tell the Israelites to turn back and encamp near Pi Hahiroth, between Migdol and the sea. They are to encamp by the sea, directly opposite Baal Zephon. Pharaoh will think, 'The Israelites are wandering around the land in confusion, hemmed in by the desert.' And I will harden Pharaoh's heart, and he will pursue them. But I will gain glory for myself through Pharaoh and all his army, and the Egyptians will know that I am the LORD." So the Israelites did this.

What was God's purpose? He created a platform for His power. What should you do when God decides to use your life and your circumstances as a platform for His power? Stand up straight. Don't cower. Dig your heels in. Hold your head up. Stand firm and watch.

When Israel found themselves in this dilemma, God already knew exactly what He was going to do. And He knows exactly what He is going to do in your situation. Watch His deliverance.

Finally, He said, "The LORD will fight for you; you need only to be still." Be still. Be at rest.

You can be free of anxiety because you know the Lord who fights for you. You can present every petition with thanksgiving. You can let His peace guard your heart and mind. His is the kingdom and the power and the glory forever.

• In the midst of circumstances that look hopeless to you, celebrate His deliverance. Write out what you know to be true about the character of God and take a firm stand on that truth.

_____

_____

_____

Distill

Quiet your thoughts. Turn your ear toward Him. What is the primary thing He has said to you? Trust what you hear Him say to you. Write it down.

_____

_____

_____

~ Day 37 ~

Delight Yourself in Him

"'In repentance and rest is your salvation, / in quietness and trust is your strength'" (Isa. 30:15). Rest. This is your strength; this is your deliverance. Quiet, trustful rest.

Discover

He said, "The knowledge of the secrets
of the kingdom of God has been given to you."
(Luke 8:10)

The kingdom belongs to God. He alone knows its secrets and He alone can disclose them. Once you enter His kingdom, He begins to teach you His secrets. He "takes the upright into his confidence" (Prov. 3:32). "The LORD confides in those who fear him" (Ps. 25:14).

When you were born into the kingdom, the kingdom was born into you (see Luke 17:20–21). All of its secrets have become accessible to you. When you live out the secrets of the kingdom of God, you will live at rest.

The kingdom is the realm of His finished work. It is living out the promises. All of the kingdom's secrets are wrapped up in one Person. All of the promises come together in one living Word. There is but one place to look for all the kingdom's treasures. In reality, the kingdom has only one secret, but this secret will change everything. It will usher you into unending soul-sabbath.

> . . . the mystery that has been kept hidden for ages and gener-
> ations, but is now disclosed to the saints. To them God has
> chosen to make known among the Gentiles the glorious riches
> of this mystery, which is Christ in you, the hope of glory.
> (Col. 1:26–27)

The secret of the kingdom is this: Christ in you. God's "Yes" living in you. God's Completed Work living in you. The fullness of him who fills everything in every way (Eph. 1:23). The One in Whom is hidden all the treasures of wisdom and knowledge living in you. Not Christ *for* you; not Christ *with* you—Christ *in* you. He is your resting place.

What decisions will you face today? Christ is in you! What challenges will confront you today? Christ is in you! What temptations will arise? Christ is in you! What fears or anxieties might surface? Christ is in you! What need might enter your life? Christ is in you!

The knowledge of the secrets of the kingdom of God has been given to you. The Sabbath, Jesus Christ, is in you.

- Think through the day or days ahead. What decisions will you be making? List them.

  _____

  _____

  _____

- What difficult situations do you anticipate dealing with? List them.

  _____

  _____

  _____

- What strained relationships will you need to face? List them.

  _____

  _____

  _____

- Now, go back to all your lists and write over them in capital letters: FOR JESUS TO HANDLE.

Distill

Quiet your thoughts. Turn your ear toward Him. What is the primary thing He has said to you? Trust what you hear Him say to you. Write it down.

_____

_____

_____

~ Day 38 ~

Delight Yourself in Him

"Lord, you establish peace for us; / all that we have accomplished you have done for us" (Isa. 26:12). All God. Everything you seem to have accomplished, He has done for you. Lean the weight of your anxiety on Him. He wants to establish peace in you. Stay quiet in His presence until His peace fills you.

Discover

For the kingdom of God is not a matter of talk but of power.
(1 Cor. 4:20)

The kingdom is not idle chatter, or empty words, or even eloquent and reasoned arguments. The kingdom of God is power.

When Christ in you becomes Christ through you, the power of God becomes operative in your world.

> Now to him who is able to do immeasurably more than all we
> ask or imagine, according to his power that is at work within
> us. (Eph. 3:20)

God is able to do more than *all* we can ask or even conceive of. When you ask God for the best thing you can think up, you ask Him for less than He can do. When you feel that your request will push the limits of His power, He wants to do more than you can imagine.

When Mary and Martha wanted Jesus to heal Lazarus, they thought they were asking all they could. When He didn't meet their expectations, they thought He had let them down. Jesus once again, however, created a platform for His power. He wanted Mary and Martha to know new things about Him. They knew He could heal the sick, but they didn't know He could raise the dead. Instead of meeting their expectations, He exceeded their expectations.

When it looks to you like God has let you down; when it looks to you like God is too late; watch! He is going to show you that He has the power to do more than you can possibly ask or imagine. The kingdom is His and the power is His and the glory is His.

The epicenter of this power is in you. "Now to him who is able to do immeasurably more than all we ask or imagine, according to *his power* that is at work *within us* (Eph. 3:20, italics added). Jesus is the power (see 1 Cor. 1:24), and Jesus is in you.

> But we have this treasure in jars of clay to show that this all-surpassing power is from God and not from us." (2 Cor. 4:7)

The Greek word for "all-surpassing" means "to throw beyond the usual mark." God's power goes beyond expectations. It surpasses every other power. He exercises this power through you. When your prayers release into circumstances a power that is beyond what you could think of or imagine, it is clear that the power is His. It is all the more astounding and breathtaking because it was poured out from a jar of clay.

* What situation have you been trying to manage? Have you been trying to convince God of the best way for Him to intervene?

_____

_____

_____

- Right now, change your prayer to this: *Father, do immeasurably more than all I can ask or imagine. Exercise Your all-surpassing power. I rest in Your sabbath.* Write down any other thoughts to God in prayer.

_____

_____

_____

Distill

Quiet your thoughts. Turn your ear toward Him. What is the primary thing He has said to you? Trust what you hear Him say to you. Write it down.

_____

_____

_____

~ Day 39 ~

Delight Yourself in Him

"My soul clings to you; your right hand upholds me" (Ps. 63:8). Cling: "to adhere to as if glued firmly" *(Webster's Dictionary).* Let the word *cling* bring into your mind thoughts and pictures that describe your soul as it clings to the Father. Rest in Him. Let Him do the work.

Discover

Glory in his holy name;
let the hearts of those who seek the LORD rejoice.
(Ps. 105:3)

Glory in His name. Hallowed be His name. We have come full circle. Jesus' prayer outline opens with honoring His name, and it comes to a close ascribing to Him honor and power and glory. The glory—the worth, the value, the weightiness—is His. He alone is worthy. In all creation, there is no other glory. "Yours is the glory."

His glory draws us to Him. Because of His surpassing worth, our hearts seek Him and His presence. It seems only natural that the lesser should long for the greater. But the astonishing truth is this as well: He longs for us. Our yearning for Him is but the shadow cast by His longing for us. He, the Glorified One, has made Himself knowable. He entered into our experience, hid the unapproachable light of His presence behind a veil of flesh, and translated Himself into Word. He desires to impart His glory to us.

Among the many layers of meaning of the word *glory* is "the radiance, the outshining, the manifested presence." His design for humans has always been that we should be His glory. When sin enters the picture, we fall short of His glory. "For all have sinned and fall short of the glory of God" (Rom. 3:23). How will He restore His glory to His people? Christ *in you,* the hope of glory.

Let's examine the concept of glory as outshining or radiance. Imagine that you and I are in a room together. An image of me registers on your brain. It's called "seeing." You are seeing me. Actually, you are not seeing *me.* You are seeing the light rays that bounce off of me. However, that's the only way for you to know what I look like. If the light in the room were off, even though I would be present, you would be unable to see me. If the lights had always been off, you might say, "No one has seen Jennifer." Then when the lights came on, you might continue, "But the light has come and has made her known. Now we see her exact image because the light has revealed her."

You may have recognized my parallel with John 1:1–5. Although the Father has always been present and active in the affairs of humans, no one had ever seen Him. Jesus, the Light, came and revealed Him. Jesus is the glory of God. Now, because Jesus is in you, operating through you, you are the glory of God. The word *glory* is completed when the worth of something is made visible. *Glory* is also the value. Through you, Jesus puts on display the glory of God.

The Father is doing a work in you that will restore your soul to its original design and its first purpose: to be the place where He displays His glory. In your life, He will glorify His name. You are the vessel, but the glory is His.

- Let the longing that you have for Him fill you. It has been awakened by the longing He has for you. Give Him yourself as a living offering. Invite Him to hallow His name through you.

_____

_____

_____

Distill

Quiet your thoughts. Turn your ear toward Him. What is the primary thing He has said to you? Trust what you hear Him say to you. Write it down.

_____

_____

_____

~ Day 40 ~

Review and Reflect

- What is the key to presenting your requests to God with thanksgiving?

_____

_____

_____

_____

- What is the secret of the kingdom? What does it change for you?

_____

_____

_____

_____

- What have you learned in these forty days about sabbathing as it directly impacts your life and the situations you are facing?

_____

_____

_____

_____

- What does this verse mean to you?

  For the kingdom of God is not a matter of talk but of power.
  (1 Cor. 4:20)

  _____

  _____

  _____

  _____

Forty-Day Review

1. What has the word *sabbath* come to mean to you?

    _____

    _____

    _____

2. What has the word *rest* come to mean to you?

    _____

    _____

    _____

3. What has the word *peace* come to mean to you?

    _____

    _____

    _____

4. In what areas of your life have you moved from *restlessness* to *rest?*

    _____

    _____

    _____

5. In a word, phrase, or sentence, summarize what each point in Jesus'
    prayer outline means to you:

    _____

    _____

Our Father in heaven, hallowed be your name.

_____

_____

Your kingdom come, your will be done on earth as it is in heaven.

_____

_____

Give us today our daily bread.

_____

_____

Forgive us our debts, as we also have forgiven our debtors.

_____

_____

Lead us not into temptation, but deliver us from the evil one.

_____

_____

For the kingdom and the power and the glory are yours.

_____

_____

SECTION 3
AN EXTENDED
RETREAT

*Create the extended retreat that meets your needs
and speaks to your longings. The important element of
your extended retreat is not what you do, but that you
are taking time away to focus on God and seek His face.*

An Extended Retreat: Introduction

You will find that as you spend forty days focusing on hearing from God, your desire for time with Him will increase. You will look for ways to spend more and more time in undistracted waiting on Him. You may want to plan an extended personal retreat.

An extended personal retreat will rejuvenate you spiritually, emotionally, and physically. It will provide the time frame and the setting in which the Father can work in you and speak to you without distraction. During this set-aside time, you can orient all of your activities and thoughts—both waking and sleeping—around Him.

An extended retreat may be a few hours, or it may be twenty-four hours. Whatever time block is realistic for you, plan for an extended time of solitude and silence. Ideally you would plan to be away from your home or work environment simply because you could escape the sense of responsibility and the pull of the work that always needs to be done. You could be beyond the reach of telephones and daily interruptions. However, if it is not possible for you to get away, you can plan for uninterrupted solitude wherever you are.

The following pages are a suggested plan for an extended retreat. You may be doing this retreat alone or with others. If you are retreating as a group, I suggest that you plan much time alone with periodic times of sharing what God is saying.

These pages are only a suggestion. Create the extended retreat that meets your needs and speaks to your longings. The important element of your extended retreat is not what you do, but that you are taking time away to focus on God and seek His face.

This retreat plan includes a series of meditations built around the Twenty-third Psalm. As you work through the meditations, do so with the expectation that God will speak to you. Be listening for Him. Complete a meditation, then go do something else—walk, relax, listen to music. Don't rush through them.

Finally, please do not feel guilty if you nap periodically during your extended retreat. This is to be a restorative time for you. As you fill your time with meditating on God's Word and allowing Him to think His thoughts in you, even when you're sleeping, your subconscious mind is still communing with the Father. In fact, specifically ask Him to continue speaking to you even while you sleep. It may be that as your soul finds deeper rest, so does your body. Scientists are beginning to discover the truth that Scripture has always held—a restful mind and a heart in repose is reflected in a person's physical body.

An Extended Retreat: Meditations

Meditation 1

Be still in the Lord's presence. With your spiritual senses, allow yourself to rest in the Shepherd's green pastures, laced with streams of still water. Let His peace rule your thoughts. Let all anxiety, fear, and worry rest on His shoulders while you enjoy His restful presence.

Open your heart to Him. Spend these moments releasing all your burdens to Him. Pray this prayer slowly and reflectively, allowing each thought to take deep root in your heart.

> Father, I want all of You. There is nothing in me that I want to hold on to more than I want to be filled with You. I release all that I am to all that You are.

Respond to Him: _____

_____

_____

_____

_____

_____

Meditation 2

Let your life become progressively more open to Him as you walk through the Twenty-third Psalm. Ask the Spirit of God—who knows the mind and heart of God and understands the deep things of God—to be your teacher and your guide.

He invites you to pour out your heart's desires to Him. Tell Him exactly what you desire.

Respond to Him: _____

_____

_____

_____

_____

_____

Meditation 3

> The LORD is my shepherd. (Ps. 23:1)

As you let this sentence reveal more of the Father to you, focus on each word. Mine its riches. The riches of the Word of God are not sitting on the surface to be skimmed off by the casual observer. Rather, they are hidden, so that the Spirit of God can reveal them personally to you.

"*The Lord* is my shepherd." Consider Who has taken you into His care and put you under His protection.

Respond to Him: _____

_____

_____

_____

_____

"The Lord *is* my shepherd." Dwell on the present-tense provision and care of the Lord. Right now, in this very instant, He is your Shepherd. He is actively shepherding you in this moment. Whatever moments lie ahead, the Lord always will be your Shepherd.

Respond to Him: _____

_____

_____

_____

_____

"The Lord is *my* shepherd." Let Him tell you about how personal His love is for you. He loves you and cares for you and provides for you individually, as if you were His only sheep.

Respond to Him:

_____

_____

_____

_____

_____

"The Lord is my *shepherd.*" He takes full responsibility for you. All you have to do is follow Him and receive His provision.

Respond to Him:

_____

_____

_____

_____

_____

_____

Meditation 4

I shall not be in want. (Ps. 23:1)

Because of who your Shepherd is, you will be well-supplied. You will never lack any good thing. Everything you need and everything you desire is in Him.

> I said to the LORD, "You are my Lord;
>   apart from you I have no good thing." (Ps. 16:2)

> Whom have I in heaven but you?
>   And earth has nothing I desire besides you. (Ps. 73:25)

> But as for me, the nearness of God is my good. (Ps. 73:28, NASB)

Is there anything for you to long for and desire except Him? He wants to be everything to you.

Respond to Him: _____

_____

_____

_____

_____

Meditation 5

> He makes me lie down in green pastures,
>   he leads me beside quiet waters, (Ps. 23:2)

Your wise and loving Shepherd provides for your rest and refreshment. The path He has marked out for you, and leads you along, will take you to a place where revival and renewal are perpetual and ongoing.

Whatever circumstances assault you; whatever difficulties confront you; whatever challenges meet you, let your soul rest in the soft, new grass, while the gentle wind of His presence caresses you. Let the peaceful sound of quiet waters soothe you.

> The LORD gives strength to his people;
>   the LORD blesses his people with peace. (Ps. 29:11)

Respond to Him: _____

_____

_____

_____

_____

_____

Meditation 6

. . . he restores my soul. (Ps. 23:3a)

He is progressively restoring your soul—your mind, your will, and your emotions—to their originally intended state. He means for your soul to be the place where His glory dwells. He means for your soul to be the place where His presence is manifested. He continually heals you from the inside out.

Let Him place His lovely, nail-pierced hand on your soul's wounds, and let the power that flows from Him restore you. Do you recall His comment as the woman with the issue of blood took hold of the hem of His garment? Even though Jesus was being thronged by crowds of people, when the woman took hold of the edge of His cloak in faith, "Jesus said, 'Someone touched me; I know that power has gone out from me'" (Luke 8:46).

He is "dressed in a robe reaching down to his feet and with a golden sash around his chest" (Rev. 1:13). Take hold of the edge of His robe—His royal robe. Bow your face to the ground. Let His power restore your soul.

Respond to Him:

_____

_____

_____

_____

_____

Meditation 7

> He guides me in paths of righteousness
>   for his name's sake. (Ps. 23:3)

He is your Way. If He is your Shepherd, then you are walking the right paths. Your safety and your security lie in Him. He guides you.

You don't have to know the way, because He knows the way. You can be at peace. You can rest in Him.

> In your unfailing love you will lead the people you have redeemed. In your strength you will guide them to your holy dwelling. (Exod. 15:13)

Have you forsaken His guidance only to find yourself on a path filled with heartache and disappointment? Have you ignored His voice and wandered onto a path that isn't right for you? He is relentlessly seeking you, calling you back. He is longing to carry you tenderly back to safety.

> For this is what the Sovereign LORD says: "I myself will search
> for my sheep and look after them." (Ezek. 34:11)

Where in your life are you not following the Shepherd? Will you return to the way He has marked out for you?

Respond to Him: _____

_____

_____

_____

_____

Meditation 8

> Even though I walk
>   through the valley of the shadow of death,
> I will fear no evil,
>   for you are with me;
> your rod and your staff,
>   they comfort me. (Ps. 23:4)

Even when the path leads you through valleys where the shadow of death hides the light, you need not dread that any evil will befall you. He is still your Shepherd—your Guide, your Protector, your Provider, your Way. Nothing has changed. Your feet may take you through the valley of the shadow of death, but let your soul rest beside the still waters.

You will not be in the valley alone. He knows all the landforms—the sudden outcroppings of rock, the precipices, the dangerous ledges. He knows because He's walked that way before. He will steer you through as carefully and gently as if He were leading a blind man along a way he has not known.

> I will lead the blind by ways they have not known,
>   along unfamiliar paths I will guide them;
> I will turn the darkness into light before them
>   and make the rough places smooth.
> These are the things I will do;
>   I will not forsake them. (Isa. 42:16)

When you lead a blind person along unfamiliar paths, you lead him step by step. When the path is familiar, the blind person can walk it unaided. The Father has set up a picture of the way He will lead you—as if you were blind and He is leading you along an unfamiliar path. Lean on Him and let Him be the Way. You will see darkness turning into light before you.

Don't be afraid of the dark. The dark valleys are as safe as the well-lit paths when the Lord is your Shepherd.

Respond to Him: _____

_____

_____

_____

_____

_____

Meditation 9

> You prepare a table before me
>> in the presence of my enemies. (Ps. 23:5)

The picture changes. Now you are an honored guest in His home. You have come under the protection of His roof. You are His responsibility.

Even when the enemy of your soul and his evil forces seem to surround you, lying in wait for you, reaching out to make you stumble; you are safe. You are safely ensconced in His dwelling place. He spreads a feast before you while your enemy looks on, frustrated, unable to reach you.

No matter what schemes your enemy has put in place, your heart can be kept in perfect peace when your mind is anchored in Him.

> You will keep in perfect peace
>> him whose mind is steadfast,
>> because he trusts in you. (Isa. 26:3)

When your mind clings to Him, you will experience complete peace. You will have *shalom* and *menuha* and *shabath*.

Respond to Him:

_____

_____

_____

_____

Meditation 10

> You anoint my head with oil;
>   my cup overflows (Ps. 23:5)

Both oil and wine, in the symbol-language of Scripture, are the Holy Spirit: the Holy Spirit in you, filling you (wine), and the Holy Spirit on you, anointing you with power for service (oil). In His house, you are filled with His Spirit and His Spirit is poured out on you.

The story of Esther is rich with symbolism. At the beginning, King Xerxes, who represents God, held a banquet. The banquet was described:

> Wine was served in goblets of gold, each one different from the other, and the royal wine was abundant, in keeping with the king's liberality. By the king's command each guest was allowed to drink in his own way, for the king instructed all the wine stewards to serve each man what he wished. (Esther 1:7–8)

Gold is symbolic of Jesus, resurrected and glorified. Do you see the goblets from which the wine was served? They were goblets of gold, "each one different from the other." Jesus comes to each person individually. Each one has his or her own personal experience with Him. He pours out the wine—the Holy Spirit—one guest at a time.

The king's instructions were: No one will be forced to drink the wine. But every man may have as much of the wine as he wants.

How much of the Holy Spirit do you desire? You may have all you want. (The outpouring on your life will only stop when you say, "Enough.")

As you sit at the King's banquet right now, lift up your voice to Him and cry out from the depths of your heart, "More wine! More wine!"

Respond to Him:

_____

_____

_____

_____

_____

The oil of anointing signifies the Holy Spirit poured out on you, equipping you with power from on high. In the Psalms we find a description of how the anointing with oil looked:

> It is like precious oil poured on the head,
>   running down on the beard,
> running down on Aaron's beard,
>   down upon the collar of his robes. (Ps. 133:2)

After the anointing, Aaron dripped with oil. As the Lord pours His Spirit out on you, your life drips with His presence and His power.

Bow before Him and ask Him to pour out His Spirit on your life.

Respond to Him:

_____

_____

_____

_____

_____

Meditation 11

> Surely goodness and love will follow me
>   all the days of my life. (Ps. 23:6)

The word translated "follow" actually means "to pursue, to run after, to chase, to hunt." His goodness and love are aggressively pursuing you. Stop running. Stand still. They will overtake you.

Will you accept all the goodness and all the love that He longs for you to experience?

Respond to Him: _____

_____

_____

_____

_____

_____

Meditation 12

> . . . and I will dwell in the house of the LORD
>   forever. (Ps. 23:6)

You have found your dwelling place: here, in the Lord's house, at home with Him. Your every need is met. Your heart's desire is fulfilled. You are kept safe. You are honored and loved.

Where else would you go? Like Peter, you have realized that He is your soul's home. "Lord, to whom shall we go? You have the words of eternal life" (John 6:68). Only in Him can you find peace and rest and soul-sabbath.

Worship Him. Give all of yourself to Him as a living offering. Honor Him. Adore Him.

Respond to Him:

_____

_____

_____

_____

_____

_____

_____

SECTION 4
RESOURCES

For Further Study

Books by Jennifer Kennedy Dean

He Restores My Soul: A Forty-Day Journey toward Personal Renewal

"Do you long to live in the Spirit's present-tense power? Do you want to know the indwelling life of Christ as your reality instead of an empty theology? Do you want Jesus to fill you with Himself? Do you want the living Lord to be someone you know, not just someone you believe in?"

With these words, readers of *He Restores My Soul: A Forty-Day Journey toward Personal Renewal* are challenged to embrace brokenness as "the ground from which all spiritual power grows." Author Jennifer Kennedy Dean takes readers through a forty-day journey that begins with brokenness and ends with overflowing power.

Live a Praying Life: Open Your Life to God's Power and Provision

"*Live a Praying Life* is one of the most practical and doctrinally sound books on prayer available. Whether studied individually or in a small group, this book will prove to be an invaluable tool. Knowing Jennifer personally, I can attest that this book is the natural outflow of her life" (Dr. Chuck Lynch, president of Living Foundation Ministries, author of *I Should Forgive, But . . .*).

A thirteen-week, in-depth interactive study on prayer addressing (1) The Purpose of Prayer, (2) The Process of Prayer, (3) The Promise of Prayer, and (4) The Practice of Prayer.

Power Praying: Prayer That Produces Results

With the release of her third volume in a trilogy on prayer, Jennifer Kennedy Dean proves once again that the truth about prayer's power lies beyond scripted, pat slogans. Dean continues to help us expand our limiting definitions of prayer and understand that prayer has no set formulas.

In this book, Dean explains the key to praying with consistent power: living moment-by-moment in the Spirit's present-tense life. She cuts through the frills to the heart of the truth as she communicates the living Jesus, the power of God working through His blood, what it means to have spiritual vision and living, active faith, and God's purpose and method for purifying His "power pray-ers."

The Praying Life: Living beyond Your Limits
"With so many books about prayer, can anything new or fresh be said? 'Probably not,' I thought as I began to read *The Praying Life*. I was happy to find this book refreshing and challenging." *(Bookstore Journal)*

Heart's Cry: Principles of Prayer
Cynthia Heald, author of *Becoming a Woman of Prayer,* quoted *Heart's Cry* (NavPress) in the company of the classic thinkers and devotional writers.

This insightful book contains twelve sections, each dealing with a scriptural principle of prayer. Each section ends with a meditation, reflection questions, and review questions. You will find *Heart's Cry* the perfect tool for personal devotionals, small group studies on prayer, or one-on-one mentoring relationships. This little book is so rich and so packed with wisdom and clear biblical teaching, it has already been called a classic.

Riches Stored in Secret Places: A Devotional Guide for Those Who Hunger after the Deep Things of God
Author Marilynn Carlson Webber calls *Riches Stored in Secret Places* "a modern devotional classic for today's Christian."

In this exciting twelve-week devotional guide, Dean shows readers how to uncover the layers of truth hidden in Scripture. Readers who long to hear God speak from His Word will find clear direction and encouragement as Dean teaches her methods for contemplative prayer, guided by God's Word. Each week readers will delve into a passage of Scripture and will practice daily journaling, prayer, and listening exercises that will start them on a lifetime journey of hearing God.

Secret Place of the Most High: A Journal for Those Who Hunger after the Deep Things of God

Journaling has long been a discipline practiced by those seeking deeper intimacy with God. In this resource, Dean gives the reader topics and thought-starters from which to journal. Beautifully designed and beautifully written, this tool will be valuable to the beginner as well as the experienced journaler. Fresh, reverent, and inspiring, *The Secret Place of the Most High* calls believers to new levels of intimacy with the Father.

Books that address forgiveness
I Should Forgive, But . . . by Chuck Lynch (Word Publishing, 1998)
You Can Work It Out by Chuck Lynch (Word Publishing, 1999)

Books that address prayer
Prayer by O. Hallesby (Augsburg Press, 1931)
Let Us Pray by Watchman Nee (Christian Fellowship Publishers, Inc., 1977)
With Christ in the School of Prayer by Andrew Murray (Fleming H. Revell, 1953)

Weekend Conferences
with Jennifer Kennedy Dean

Live a Praying Life: Open Your Life to God's Power and Provision

An in-depth study of prayer: the *purpose* of prayer, the *process* of prayer, the *promise* of prayer, the *practice* of prayer. This conference deals with the universal questions about prayer in a fresh, clear, and biblically sound manner. If God is sovereign, why do we pray? How can prayer produce change on the earth? What does the phrase "stand in the gap" mean? Why are there sometimes long delays between request and answer? This study is packed with important insights on how to make prayer a life rather than an activity.

Power Praying: Prayer That Produces Results

A follow-up study to *Live a Praying Life* (or this study can stand alone). This study will teach you how to live and pray with the kind of power promised in Scripture. You will learn the avenues, clarified in God's Word, through which the power of God becomes available to the believing pray-er. Contains powerful teaching on the blood of Jesus, spiritual vision, active faith, God's method and purpose for purifying His people, and the Spirit's present-tense power.

The Praying Woman: Impacting Her World

This study teaches women how to develop such a rich inner life of prayer that it spills out to those around her.

He Restores My Soul

Based on the book of the same name. Participants will learn how God is using every moment of every day to restore our souls to be the place where His glory dwells. Discover the power of the indwelling Christ as He releases "the power of His resurrection" in you.

Author and Weekend Conference Information:

The Praying Life Foundation
P.O. Box 62
Blue Springs, MO 64013
jenniferkdean@prayinglife.org
www.prayinglife.org
(888) 844–6647 or (816) 228–8899
Fax: (816) 228–0925

Endnotes

1. Andrew Murray, *The Secret of Believing Prayer* (Minneapolis, MN: Bethany Fellowship, Inc., 1980), 74–75.

2. Everett Fox, *The Five Books of Moses,* The Schocken Bible Volume 1, (New York: Schocken Books, 1997), p. 17.

3. *Shabbatu,* the noun in Babylonian, means "a cycle in a chronological sense, the day on which the moon completes its cycle."

4. Abraham Joshua Heschel, *The Sabbath* (Toronto: HarperCollins Canada Ltd, 1951), 22–23.

5. James S. Stewart, *The Life and Teaching of Jesus Christ* (Nashville, TN: Abingdon Press, 1957), 89.

6. Oswald Chambers, *Christian Disciplines* (Grand Rapids, MI: Chosen Books, 1985), 41.

7. Jennifer Kennedy Dean, *Secret Place of the Most High* (Birmingham, AL: New Hope, 1997), 140, 144.

8. Chambers, *Christian Disciplines*, 40.

9. Marvin R. Vincent, D.D., *Vincent's Word Studies of the New Testament* (Peabody, MA: Henderson Publishers, 1984), 261. See also *The Amplified Bible,* Luke 1:37.

10. Jennifer Kennedy Dean, *Secret Place of the Most High* (Birmingham, AL: New Hope, 1996), 29.

11. A phrase used in the penal system to describe a person who has received a death sentence. He or she is alive, but death is certain.

12. E. M. Bounds, *The Necessity of Prayer.*

13. Jennifer Kennedy Dean, *Power Praying: Prayer That Produces Results* (Mukilteo, WA: Winepress Publishing, 1997), 87–88.

14. F. Brook, quoted by Oswald Chambers, *Christian Disciplines* (Grand Rapids, MI: Chosen Books, 1985), 64.

15. Spiros Zodhiates, *The Complete Word Study Dictionary* (Chattanooga, TN: AMG Publishers, 1992), 1265.

16. This phrase is not found in the earliest manuscripts, and most updated translations omit it or have it in footnote form. It apparently was added by the early church as they used this prayer for corporate worship. However, it is certainly not contradictory to any of Jesus' teachings on prayer. In fact, it is right in line with them. It has been a meaningful part of this passage for many hundreds of years.